the structure of music: *a listener's guide*

The Noonday Press

a subsidiary of

Farrar, Straus & Giroux
New York

THE STRUCTURE OF MUSIC: *a listener's guide*

by Robert Erickson

a study of music in terms of melody and counterpoint

with an introduction by Virgil Thomson

COUNTERPOINT, WHAT IS IT? 3

CONTENTS

'NTRODUCTION

Music, like anything else, consists of raw materials and of construction. The raw materials of music are three—rhythm, melody and harmony. Construction, or the need for cohesiveness, has developed two major techniques in the last eight centuries—counterpoint and orchestration. Today these five principles govern all music. Three of them—rhythm, melody and harmony are basic elements and cannot be taught easily. The other two are mere procedures and present no insoluble problem to pedagogy.

I place the elements in the above order because that must have been the order of their discovery. Rhythm can exist alone; the others cannot. But rhythm can exist alone only if the instrument of it is a percussive one, not a source of continuous sound. If the sound is steady, rhythm itself requires that the pitch be varied. Thus melody is born of rhythm's needs.

Harmony is born out of melody through the acoustical phenomenon of reverberation. When one pitch overlaps another, you have an interval vertically arranged. When, through accident or design, several tunes are heard at once, you have lots of intervals vertically arranged; and the ordering of them into harmony becomes needful. So does their ordering into rhythm and meter. This dual ordering produces counterpoint.

But counterpoint is not a thing in itself. It is nothing more than the ordering of multiple melodies into a clear rhythmic and harmonic relation. And orchestration, or scoring, is a further exploitation of acoustical phenomena that clarifies (by contrasts of range and color) and emphasizes (by harmonic supports and percussive underpinnings) the generative elements.

Counterpoint (and orchestration too) can point up a tune and its harmonic implications either by contrast or by similarity. A fugal theme and its countersubject are usually marked by dissimilarity of rhythmic and melodic structure. The practice of moving these themes about, however, from voice to voice in fugal writing, produces a homogeneous contrapuntal texture not essentially different from those of Late Mediaeval and Renaissance choral music, which deal chiefly in thematic imitation. This kind of counterpoint I call non-differentiated, although the voices may set one another off by contrast from moment to moment, in the long run they all perform melodies of identical character.

Contrapuntal voices of contrasted character have existed since first the *cantus firmus* was employed. And from the expressed *cantus firmus,* through variations over a ground bass to our use of ostinato in boogie-woogie, this possibility of differentiation has been dramatized by composers. The full use of keyboard, wind and stringed instruments all at the same time, makes differentiation necessary, since a flute and a trumpet, a harp and a trombone are not at their best playing identical figures. Even a man's bass voice and a high soprano have more freedom and more character when they proceed in duet by contrast than by conformity.

Opera has long achieved its most striking effects through differentiated writing, vocal and instrumental. In the great ensemble numbers of Mozart, Rossini, Donizetti and Verdi each character sings in character. Lucia di Lammermoor, at the height of the famous sextet, utters her cries of despair at the dominant and in syncopation. Donna Elvira in the Quartet from *Don Giovanni* insists, in her warning to Donna Anna, by means of assertive arpeggios, which her seducer explains away as proof of her unreason. All this makes for drama, which is ever a play of contrasts.

The quality of drama in Beethoven's and Schubert's symphonies, the power of evoking a scene or landscape that is the glory of Wagner, Strauss and Debussy, come from pitting the string body of an orchestra against the woodwinds and the brasses and the drums in a multiple, often a warring, antiphony. Music after Bach was not, as is commonly thought, a retreat from counterpoint. It was a progress from non-differentiated, homogeneous counterpoint into a highly differentiated, or dramatized, counterpoint.

In our century the school of Paris has remained faithful, on the whole, to dramatic and picturesque exploitations of the contrapuntal principle. Their polyrhythmics and dual harmonies are a logical extension of that principle. The school of Vienna, on the other hand, has executed an impressive return (possibly a retreat) to non-differentiated counterpoint in its most complete form, which is the canon. Even key contrasts have been abandoned for an atonal chromatic continuum in which all the voices float under an equalized, loose-as-possible harmonic tension. Rhythm, with these composers, is also fluid and, after the manner of Viennese rubato, subjective, visceral, seemingly spontaneous.

Whether the future will see a complete fusion of the two schools is not yet clear, though efforts in that direction are a dominant theme of post-war European music. What is clear already is that the music of the Viennese school, which, save for its non-tonal thorough-bass, is constructed along the lines of classical counterpoint, yields itself more easily to analysis by classical methods than does that of Paris, at best that of pre-war Paris. It is no doubt for this reason that Robert Erickson's *The Structure of Music* can dissect with equal effectiveness a Mass by Okeghem, a quartet by Mozart and a symphony of Anton Webern.

This uncommonly enlightened book tells the history of music through the history of counterpoint, chiefly of non-differentiated counterpoint. It might have been told as well through the history of scoring. For music's best story is the story of its secondary techniques. Rhythm, melody and harmony are too dynamic to have a clear history. Explaining them systematically is out of the question. Teaching them at all is a precarious effort. But counterpoint and scoring are solid subjects in any music school's curriculum. Professionals can master them; laymen can understand. As a layman's guide to listening, Mr. Erickson's book offers a penetrating experience of music through the examination of a musical procedure that has from its beginning been one of the two domains in which composers have worked with complete awareness of what they were up to and how they were doing it.

VIRGIL THOMSON

the structure of music: *a listener's guide*

COUNTERPOINT, WHAT IS IT?

Our modern word counterpoint comes directly from the latin *punctus contra punctum.* The basic meaning of the phrase, which translates to "point against point," or "note against note," refers specifically to one of the dimensions of polyphonic (many voiced) music. Notes are sounded against notes—that is to say, heard together. If we imagine the dots in the illustration on page 4 to represent notes, those placed on a vertical line would be the "points against points," a group of notes sounding simultaneously. In modern terms, simply a chord.

But there is another dimension in polyphonic music; the melodic. We can represent it visually by drawing horizontal connecting lines in our system of points. When music is composed in such a way that the melodic-horizontal dimension is thrown into re-

Vertical—Chords

lief and given a primary role we call it contrapuntal music or counterpoint.

Horizontal—Melodies

In contrapuntal music the lines of melody are of primary interest, but this does not mean that the vertical dimension ceases to exist. All polyphony has the two dimensions. Although music which is chord centered (vertical) must necessarily be very different from music which is melody centered (horizontal), nevertheless there is in all counterpoint constant

the structure of music

interplay between the vertical-chordal and the linear-horizontal. The lines of melody sounding together produce the vertical dimension, but the melodies can hardly skip along independently with no regard for how they sound with each other. Nor can the vertical-chordal dimension dictate every movement of the melodies. Somehow an aesthetic balance between the two dimensions must be created. A definition of counterpoint such as Ernst Kurth's, "The essence of the theory of counterpoint is how two or more lines can unfold simultaneously in the most unrestrained melodic development, not by means of the chords but in spite of them," seems excellent, especially as an antidote to the views of some of the writers of the past century who viewed counterpoint as little more than a matter of getting from chord to chord. It emphasizes vigorously that counterpoint is melody centered; that the melodic movements, not the harmonic progressions from chord to chord, create the shape and character of the music. Unfortunately it leaves the impression that in contrapuntal music the chords are a cumbersome baggage which the composer would dispense with if he could. The truth is that in good counterpoint the vertical events are as carefully controlled by the composer as the melodic movements. Chords are used to help define points of rest and climax, stressed and unstressed beats, and to help the forward flow of the music in a multitude of ways. The vertical dimension cannot be dispensed with, and counterpoint written "in spite of the chords" will certainly sound bad.

COUNTERPOINT, WHAT IS IT?

Although the two dimensions can hardly exist independently of one another in polyphonic music, one or the other may be of primary importance. To illustrate

String Quartet Opus 20 #6, Joseph Haydn

the essential differences between vertical and horizontal musical styles let us discuss two extreme examples.

Haydn wrote a goodly amount of contrapuntal music, but the opening of his *Sun Quartet,* Opus 20 #6, shows a predominantly vertical organization.

Throughout the whole passage the melody is determined by the underlying chords. The top line is in fact nothing more than a melodic breaking up of the underlying chord: the tones of the melody are limited to those contained in the chord itself. The melody uses these tones in various rhythmic shapes in order to add to the musical interest, its function being to decorate the chords by splitting them up prismatically, stringing them out in time in order to keep the music moving forward. This is clearly a chordal, or chord determined, melody.

Play through each of the other three parts. You will see that neither the second violin nor the viola nor the cello has an independent line of melody. These parts were not meant to carry melodic interest. Each is an element in a chordal organization and is meaningless by itself. When played together the various instruments produce chords which move from one to the other in a meaningful way. The coherence and structure of the music is guaranteed primarily by relations between the chords, not by melodic elements.

Now examine the opening of Contrapunctus VIII from Bach's *Art of Fugue.* Here all is melody. From beginning to end each independent voice has its own musical integrity. The melodies are not chord determined as in the Haydn example; the intervallic tensions between the tones themselves are used to create, develop, and release melodic energy. Chords, important though they are to the total sense of the music, have been arrived at melodically. The composer has conceived of them, not as solid and inde-

Contrapunctus VIII, Art of Fugue, J. S. Bach

pendent masses of sound, but more as meeting places or assemblies of tones. Each tone has come from some place before the meeting and is going somewhere after it is over. The chords produced by such meetings are "incidental" in the sense that the basic structure of the music does not depend upon them as it did in the Haydn example. Here the musical structure is a product of the expansion and development of the several interrelated melodic lines.

While it is well to remember that in most music the distinction between vertical and linear organization cannot be drawn so sharply, there are large bodies of music which are clearly in one or the other of the two categories. An enormous wealth of contrapuntal music from the 14th, 15th and 16th centuries has only recently begun to attract the attention it deserves. The Baroque period, dominated by J. S. Bach, presents another great body of contrapuntal music. Contrapuntal art declined somewhat in the late 18th and 19th centuries, although we have many works in various contrapuntal forms by Haydn, Mozart, Beethoven and Brahms. Since 1900 composers have shown a new interest in linear organization, and now many of them write in contrapuntal idioms of various types.

However, an overwhelming proportion of the music with which we are most familiar—the songs, operas, symphonies, sonatas, dances etc., of the 18th and 19th century Classic and Romantic composers—is chord-centered. Even our popular tunes, our functional music for dancing, movies, radio and television, our cowboy songs and spirituals, are written in a homophonic idiom. We are so familiar with that idiom that we are likely to take it for granted, sometimes to the point of feeling that homophony is a "natural" form of musical expression, more "natural" at any rate than counterpoint, where the composer "only manipulates melodies." The claim has been made that we cannot even hear counterpoint because it is impossible to listen to several melodies at the same time.

While it is probably true that the ear and mind cannot attend equally to simultaneous musical events, this view betrays a lack of knowledge about how we listen to music. Even in a simple song with accompaniment, we have more than one thing to follow. Although the single strand of melody is the primary object of our attention there is also a background to it, the accompaniment. Do we hear the background? Of course we do. We hear the accompaniment and the melody as a whole, but our attention constantly flickers back and forth through the musical texture.

From this it is easy to see that one can listen to several different melodies unfolding simultaneously. We do not listen to all of the parts with the same degree of concentration all of the time, any more than we stare exclusively at some particular point in a painting which we are looking at. On the contrary, the attention flickers from voice to voice in the counterpoint, focusing sharply on different parts from moment to moment, while relegating others to the background. It is true that in listening to contrapuntal music, where the relation between foreground and background is continually shifting about, more work is often required from the ear and mind than in following a simple tune with accompaniment. The attention cannot drift along lazily with a single line of melody. The ear and mind must be active. The attention must follow the sense of the music, moving nimbly back and forth throughout the whole musical fabric from motive to motive, accent to accent, theme to theme, line to line.

If we must follow the interweaving of independent melodic strands when we listen, and if contrapuntal music is in essence horizontal rather than vertical, then we must look first to melody, that most essential ingredient of music, if we wish to understand contrapuntal processes and techniques. For melody is the vital element. Without it the music would be meaningless.

MELODY

Scholars have investigated every conceivable aspect of music. They have measured the vibrato in the singing voice; they have systematized the chord progressions used by composers; they have explored the relationships between music's parts and members to the end that hundreds of musical forms and sub-forms are now catalogued and categorized. The search for the principles underlying the variety of surface appearance in music has resulted in an imposing number of musical laws, rules and recipes. Further distilled, these rules and laws serve as the basis of textbooks used to teach young musicians their craft. There seem to be textbooks about everything—dozens of them. There are even textbooks which purport to teach a singer how to breathe! Why, then, in a world glutted with textbooks, are there so few about melody?

The making of a melody is too personal a thing. It is a direct and unified act, like that of an artist when he draws a line, for which no prescription or formula can be given. To be sure there are no prescriptions or formulas for the other components of music either. There is no single "right way" to make a modulation from one key to another; nor is there a recipe for making a sonata-allegro form, even though many textbooks give that impression. Music of value always proves to have been freshly conceived, not written "by the book."

Nevertheless, one can more easily abstract general principles from other aspects of music, such as harmony, orchestration, etc., than melody. The composer's unique personal qualities are concentrated in his melodies, and the very individuality which makes his melodies aesthetically valuable makes it all the more difficult to abstract general principles from his practice.

With this in mind, we can see that any generalizations about melody must necessarily be very broad and therefore imperfect. But if we are to find any principles at all, simply to learn some of the ways in which melodies are constructed, we must use a net of not too fine a mesh, knowing that the unique, the individual and personal, in a word the something that makes the melody alive, can never be caught with words.

Every melody has two fundamental characteristics, pitch and duration. Every melody moves spatially up and down, and forward in time. In order to discuss the up and down qualities without the interference of rhythmic features, let us imagine a pitch skeleton for the theme of Bach's Fugue in G Major from the Well-Tempered Clavier. Since neither note

Fugue in G Major, J. S. Bach

The melody rises gradually, pushing first toward the A and B, then relaxes and gathers new force for the skip up to the C; the pattern of "relax, gather force, for the skip" is repeated before the skip to the highest note, E. After reiterating the E the melody descends again.

length nor measure is indicated, the various pitches merely follow one another to produce a meandering curve. Even without benefit of any rhythmic profile the curve has a certain shapeliness and unity, produced by the over-all tendency toward and away from the high note, E.

If you sing or play this rhythmically neutral fragment without regard for any regulating measure bar, you will discover a most interesting fact: the highest notes seem to acquire a certain extra weight. The A and B at the beginning of the melody are each higher than their neighbors; likewise the high C and E. This weightiness or stress is called tonic accent.

Accent by reason of height is common to language too. In speaking, when we wish to emphasize something we raise the pitch of our voices; certain languages even have accent signs indicating rising or falling inflections for words. For example, the word "hee-haw," imitating a donkey's bray, has two syllables of different pitch, the higher "hee" being the accented syllable. Higher pitch produces accent because we feel high tones to be more intense than lower tones, and because more physiological effort has to be expended to produce higher tones.

There is, however, both in music and language a curious "reversed tonic accent." Here the lowest instead of the highest notes get the stress. The effect in language of deepening the voice in order to emphasize a word or phrase to give it weight or power, is paralleled exactly in music. The excerpt from the fourth movement of the *Lyric Suite* by Alban Berg

Lyric Suite, Alban Berg

The high B flat in the first measure clearly carries an accent. The D and E flat in the third measure are accented also, and in the fourth and fifth measures the A and the C. Even the G at the beginning of the sixth measure and the A flat at the end of that measure acquire accents by being slightly higher in pitch than their neighbors. The second, sixth, and last measures contain reversed tonic accents. The F# in measure two and the F in measure six attract accents, and the final note of the example owes its special weight and definiteness to the reversed tonic accent.

contains both tonic accents and reversed tonic accents.

Ordinarily we interpret changes of pitch spatially. When a melody moves from note to note we hear it going higher or lower. If the melody moves within a narrow range we hear it as movement within a small space, and if it moves throughout a wide range, as does the excerpt from the Berg *Lyric Suite,* we interpret this as a large or wide space. Compare the Berg excerpt with the excerpt from Bartok's "Music for Strings, Percussion and Celeste." The difference in

Music for String Instruments, Percussion and Celeste, Bela Bartok

aesthetic effect is due in great part to the differences in range. Berg sweeps his melody through a range of more than two actaves; Bartok uses a range of only a perfect fifth.

Melody can express not only up and down, wide and narrow, but even the particular quality of the spatial movement. Motion upward might be stepwise (conjunct) as in the Bartok excerpt, or it might be mainly by skip (disjunct) as in the Berg melody. Melodies which contain many disjunct intervals feel angular and full of tension. Conjunct movement feels more relaxed. Usually melodies make use of both types of motion—the Bach melody already discussed is typical.

MELODY

Fugue in G Major, J. S. Bach

The character of the spatial up or down movement depends, then, not only upon the range of the melody but upon the kind of melodic intervals, steps or skips, which make it up. Generally speaking, the larger the skip the greater the tension between the two tones. In Bach's theme the two large skips in measures two and three create much more tension than the stepwise motion which precedes and follows them. Again, in Berg's melody where almost all of the intervals are skips, the larger skips create the greater tension.

THE RHYTHM SKELETON

The spatial motion from note to note up and down must necessarily take place in time. Are all of the tones of equal length? If not, what is their relation with each other? Which notes are accented and what is the underlying accent pattern, if any? These ques-

Fugue in G Major, J. S. Bach

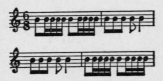

the structure of music

tions belong to the durational side of melody. Let us take them up one at a time.

Most melodies move along irregularly in time; some notes are held longer than others. In the rhythm skeleton of Bach's theme there are three different note lengths, quarter, eighth and sixteenth. These note lengths appear in various patterns, ♪♫♫ and ♫♪♪, which combine to produce the overall rhythm skeleton of the melody.

Rhythmic patterns of long and short notes can hardly be discussed apart from accent. The reason lies in another musical principle as fundamental as the tonic accent: long notes always attract accent. Perhaps it is incorrect to say that the note attracts an accent; it is our attention which is attracted, and we feel the longer notes as having more importance or musical weight than neighboring shorter ones. Our ears and minds always try to organize sounds into accent patterns. When we hear a clock making a "tíck-tŏck" we are organizing the sound into such an accent pattern. The fact that if we try we can hear the same clock going "tŏck-tíck" proves that our minds do the organizing.

"Tock" and "tick" are syllables of roughly equal length. To illustrate the long note accent say the phrase, "túm tă túm tă túm tă túm." The long syllable, "tum," attracts the accent. If you try to reverse the process by saying "tŭm tá tŭm tá tŭm tá," you will find it necessary to artificially lengthen the "ta" to "taaa." Similarly if the pattern ♩♩♩♩♩♩ is played or hummed with no attempt to give either note value any special accentual push, the longer note will appear to be relatively accented and the shorter note will feel relatively unaccented. This accent of length (agogic accent) is one of the elements of Bach's theme. The ♪ of  is accented every time it appears. But in measures two and three of the

Fugue in G Major, J. S. Bach

same example the ♪ gets the accent only on first beats of the measure. The longer ♩ at the end of measures two and three attracts an even stronger accent. In these two measures both tonic accents and agogic accents are used to throw tones into relief. The combination of the two types of accent is illustrated in Berg's theme too, where the highest note is almost always the longest note among its neighbors.

The longest note doesn't always get the accent. An accent pattern is often implied through the use of bar line, measure and time signature. For example in common 4/4 time, march time with its ONE, two, *three,* four, the first quarter note of every measure is

customarily accented. The third quarter note of the measure receives a subsidiary accent. In 3/4 time, waltz time, the first quarter note beat of the measure receives an accent and the last two beats are un-accented. In 6/8 time the first and fourth eighth notes carry accents and all the other beats are unaccented.

Obviously such patterns of strong and weak beats perform a powerful, almost dictatorial, regularizing function. Dance music, march music, and all musical types which depend upon a regularly recurring accent pattern can be fitted into such regular measures quite easily, but the "tyranny of the bar line" about which composers have so often complained is a very real problem. How can melodies expand freely and individually if on the first beat of every measure they must willy-nilly produce an accent? How can contrasting lines be opposed to one another if they are allowed no freedom of accent?

The bar line regulates the accent pattern but not quite so rigidly as one might think. A glance at any contrapuntal music provides proof that not all first beats are accented. Even in the tonal music of the 18th and 19th centuries, when the "tyranny of the bar line" reigned, we find that contrapuntal music maintained a certain restricted freedom with regard to accent. Examine Bach's theme once again. The 6/8 time signature implies an accent on the first and fourth eighth notes of the measure, but in measures two and three the implied accent on the fourth eighth note has been displaced—moved to a beat which would not ordinarily receive an accent. From this it is apparent that although measure and time signature

Fugue in G Major, J. S. Bach

may indicate an implied pattern of accented and unaccented beats, it is by no means usual in contrapuntal music to have every potential accent actually realized.

Of course, if too many accents are displaced the underlying accent pattern cannot be felt. One feels no regular accent pattern at all in the freely flowing motion of the Bartok excerpt. The measure bars seem

Music for String Instruments, Percussion and Celeste, Bela Bartok

to be a mere bookkeeping mechanism, a way of grouping notes together so the performer can read them easily. There is not even a regular sequence of like measures; instead, a measure of 8/8 is followed by 12/8, 8/8 and 7/8. Apparently Bartok's attitude toward the measure is completely different from

Bach's. There are not even any accent displacements in the ordinary sense; how can an accent be displaced when no implied accent pattern has been set up?

But look again. What is the meaning of those dotted bar lines? Aren't they the vestigial remains of the once tyrannical bar? Doesn't the composer imply through their use that the first beat following each of the bars and dotted bars carries an implied accent of some sort? If we examine the measure segments produced by the dotted bars we see that the composer has in effect articulated the music into groups of either two eigthth notes, three eighth notes, or four eighth notes. He has retained one advantage of having measure bars: the opportunity to indicate an implied accent. He has rid himself of the tyranny of the bar line because his system of barring carries no implication of any regular accent pattern.

Bartok's ingenious solution to the problem of bar accent and time signature is representative of many which modern composers have attempted. Any contrapuntal music must allow for complementary and even opposing and contradictory accents between the various lines. Our notation system, which is so admirably suited to homophonic music, needs many improvements, perhaps complete overhauling, before it can convey simply and adequately the kind of irregularly accented melodic motion so common today. In the meantime, composers continue to use the traditional means of notation, supplementing them in various ways with dotted bar lines, measures of varying length and special accent markings.

Any melody is analogous to a moving line. The line is strictly speaking never continuous; there is always a jump from tone to tone, and the visual analogy of a series of dots producing the effect of a line would be more accurate. Certain melodies are, like the hatched lines in an etching, broken into many discontinuous segments; others sound smooth and unbroken. Interestingly enough, melodies which are angular are often discontinuous, and melodies which are continuous are often conjunct and curvilinear.

Disjunct melodic movement produces tension, and generally speaking, the more skips the melody has the more tension will be created. Skips in a melody cannot continue in the same direction indefinitely and whenever they change direction they necessarily produce melodic tension. We feel the line as a moving body with the physical characteristics of weight, momentum, and inertia. If a line starts in one direction we expect it to continue its momentum in that direction unless it meets some obstacle or reaches a goal. When the line changes direction often, when as in the Webern melody below, it moves like a football player running through a scattered field of opponents, we feel strong tensions because of the force exerted to overcome the momentum in the original direction. If the tension created by constant changes of direction is reinforced by disjunct motion from pitch to pitch and by disjunct motion in time, an extraordinary effect of excitement and intensity, such as permeates the Webern melody, results.

Quartet for Violin, Clarinet, Tenor-Saxophone and Piano, Op. 22, Anton Webern

How different the following melody from the *"Agnus Dei"* of Okeghem's *Missa Prolationum.* Except for the single rest (even when singing Okeghem the singers had to breathe) the melody has no break

Angus Dei from Missa Prolationum, Johannes Okeghem

from beginning to end. The smooth conjunct curvilinear flow has an entirely different expressive character from Webern's melody. There are only five small skips in the whole line; all the other motion is stepwise. The momentum, once under way, is never roughly interrupted, and even the smaller melodic movements run smoothly toward melodic goals—high notes and low notes—without the sudden shocks and tensions typical of the Webern melody.

While it may be not quite fair to compare melodies of composers with such completely different styles, the principle involved, the expressive effect of continuity and discontinuity, is made dramatically obvious. That the principle holds true even in melodies within the same general style may be demonstrated by comparing Webern's melody with one by Schoenberg, from his "Serenade," Opus 24.

Serenade, Op. 24, A. Schoenberg

© 1924 and 1952 by William Hansen, Copenhagen.

The range of Schoenberg's melody is two and one half octaves; melodically it is almost as disjunct as the Webern, and there are just about as many angular direction changes. Yet its overall effect is much smoother than that of Webern because it moves much more continuously. To be sure, the smoothness is reinforced by the articulation—slurs instead of staccato markings, no mixing of plucked and bowed sounds, narrower dynamic range, etc., but even when these important elements are considered, one feels that basic to the expressive effect of each is the melodic continuity or lack of it.

MUSICAL GRAVITY

Melodies go up and down, they go forward in time, but where do they go? Do they move purposefully? If they move purposefully, what or where are their goals?

All melodies, regardless of their particular style, move toward and away from points of relative tension and relative rest. Movement toward a point of tension gives purpose and direction to the line, as does movement toward a point of rest. In any musical composition, as in a novel, there are many "sentences." The musical sentences gain point and coherence by having climax points and cadences, points of rest. But the composition as a whole should have an over-all climax too, to unify and order all the musical happenings. The individual climaxes of the separate musical phrases should be related to one another so that they always point toward this over-all climax, just as all the events in a novel tend toward a *dénouement*. The melodic phrase or sentence is always part of a larger organization which finally determines its particular shape and character. Strictly speaking, we always should think of the phrase in relation to the whole, but this is impractical until we gather some understanding of how phrases work singly. So when we discuss purpose in melody, where it goes and what its goal is, we ought to investigate first the phrase or sentence, then the place of the phrase within the total organization.

Tension points are usually higher than other parts of the melody. We touched upon this fact in the discussion about tonic accent, but there are interesting general relations between high notes and tension. To understand these relations we should think for a moment about the "law" of musical gravity. There is such a law! Naturally it has more exceptions in experience than Newton's famous law. In the world of melody it is not always true that "everything that goes up has to come down"; but Newton's law is not universally applicable either since the advent of Einstein and the new physics.

Put musically, movement upward is felt as strain, tension, lifting against a downward pull. Phrases push upward to a high point, then move downward to a lower point of relative relaxation and rest. Remember, a melodic line is analogous to a moving body. If it exhibits inertia and momentum it must have weight too. The weight, inertia and momentum are of course those of our own bodies. We project our feeling for and about physical motion upon the melodic line. *We* push to the high note; *we* skip, slide, or fall to a lower note.

The way in which the melody reaches the high point, and the position of the high point in relation to the rest of the phrase is in practice extremely varied. Musicologists have even found certain types of phrases typical of particular historical styles and of certain composers working within those styles. By far the most usual phrase formation in Gregorian chant is a curve which could be graphically illustrated as  . The phrase mounts quickly to its highest point, then glides gently downward, not in a straight line, but with small to and fro motions, like a falling leaf.

Fugue in G Major, J. S. Bach

This pattern is reversed in many of Bach's melodies. The Bach theme which we examined earlier shows a gradual ascent to the high point of the phrase, then a rapid falling away. The effect is often of a slow buildup of energy which, at the high point of the phrase, is suddenly released, sometimes almost explosively. Some typical forms follow.

Well Tempered Clavier, Prelude in D Major, J. S. Bach

Well Tempered Clavier, Prelude in A Major, J. S. Bach

Well Tempered Clavier, Prelude in B Major, J. S. Bach

Well Tempered Clavier, Prelude in A Minor, J. S. Bach

Well Tempered Clavier, Fugue in A Minor, J. S. Bach

A more complex type of curve moves downward to gain momentum before it begins the climb to the top of the phrase. We run down a hill in order more easily to gain the slope ahead. The relaxation of downward motion is converted into a gathering of energy. This type of melodic motion is like the windup of a pitcher in that its whole purpose is to create melodic energy, just as the pitcher's windup exists only to put power into the delivery of the ball. A fragment from the Presto of Bach's Partita #1 in B minor for solo violin will serve as an illustration.

Presto from Partita #1 in B Minor for Solo Violin, J. S. Bach

Of course there are many many melodies which are not easily fitted into categories. Rarely is a musical phrase a bald . The phrase usually has other tension points which focus and direct the melodic energy toward its climactic point. Therefore a truer image might look like:

The single highest note expresses the greatest tension of the phrase, the full extent to which the melodic energy can attain against the gravitational pull. Sometimes the highest note is reiterated; even when there is no single high note there is almost always a high area, a climactic region, in the phrase. Such climactic points are the phrase's most important tones; all the other notes owe their existence to and are pointed toward them. More than any other single factor they give the melodic line direction and contour. Without such tension points the melody would move aimlessly, without direction or purpose.

Relaxation of the tension is accomplished in two ways: through downward melodic motions, and through the use of cadences and resting points of various types. We feel downward motion as relaxation because the movement is with, not against, the force of musical gravity. Downward movements, because they are not associated with strain against gravity, attract proportionately less attention, and are felt as less "active" than upward motions.

There are resting places, cadences of one kind or another, in all melodies. The word itself is expressive of their function: *cadere*, the Latin root word means literally, "to fall." The final note of the excerpt from Bach's Four Duets, #1, is an obvious cadence point, as is the last syllable of the word, *salve*, in the excerpt

Four Duets, J. S. Bach

from Dufay's motet, *"Ave Regina Coelorum,"* and the last syllable of the word *sancta* in the same example.

Motet, Ave Regina Coelorum, Guillaume Dufay

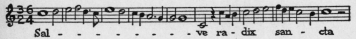

Sal - - - - - - - - - ve ra - dix san - cta

Less obvious types of melodic resting points, which are nevertheless important to the melodic line, may be seen in these same examples. The melody from the Bach Four Duets is articulated into segments by short rests. In each segment the note just preceding the rest is a point of rest, a melodic cadence. See how Bach uses these melodic cadences to relate phrase to phrase and part to whole.

More subtle are the resting points which are really "taking off" points. The word cadence is almost too definite to apply to them, but they have a great deal to do with the spring and flexibility, or lack of it, in the line. Listen for example, to the first segment of a melody from Obrecht's *Tandernaken.*

We have seen how melodic tension is created by upward movements and released by downward movements. Every melody contains both sorts, but sometimes one, sometimes the other, predominates. In

Tandernaken, Obrecht

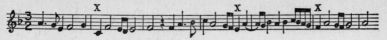

The lowest note, C, is a resting point which serves as a springboard for the leap up to the following F. The E in the next segment (also marked with an X) has a similar function. In each case the leap is made to a note which has both an agogic and a tonic accent.

Bach's melodies it is the upward push, the energetic drive to the climactic point which is especially developed and elaborated. In Gregorian chant the opposite is true: the upward movements are quickly effected and the main substance of the melody is concentrated in the delicately balanced, oscillating downward motions. Palestrina's elegant, neutral style adheres to an almost mathematical balance of upward and downward motions. In the following melody from his madrigal, *"Alla riva del Tebro,"* the melody begins and ends on C. Its range is from low F to high G, the highest note being used only once. Movements above the center tone, C, are approximately equal to movements below. Small movements up are followed by small movements down. A large upward movement, such as a skip, is compensated for by conjunct motion in the opposite direction. The relaxing stepwise motion quickly draws the attention away from the tension point, softening its impact and incorporating it into the graceful and urbanely sophisticated melodic line.

MELODY

Madrigal, Alla riva del Tebro, Palestrina

Al - la ri-va del teb-ro   gio - va-net - to vid'- io, va - go   pas-

tor   va - go pa-sto - re gio-va-net-to vid'-io va-go pa - - sto - re,

© Harvard University Press

INTERVAL TENSION

Nothing is more important to the creation of areas of melodic tension and repose than intervallic tensions, the tensions which exist between the intervals themselves. Some melodic intervals are inherently more dynamic than others. From the point of view of musical gravity, larger skips produce more tension than smaller skips. Therefore a chart from unison to skip of the 10th ought to show a steady rise in tension from the smaller to the larger intervals.

But if you play over the intervals you will hear that there is no such steady rise in tension. Some of the smaller intervals create more tension than some

of the larger ones. Spatial distance between tones is obviously not the only factor. The character of the relation between the two tones of the interval itself is involved. If you play the intervals, listening carefully for differences in tension, you will probably agree that the most static intervals are those marked P, and the most dynamic those marked D. Complete public agreement about which intervals are most tense and which are most relaxed can never be attained.

One person may accept as sounding "good" the very interval which sounds "bad" to another ear. The words, "good," "bad," "consonance," "dissonance," "concord" and "discord" are unfortunately used more or less indiscriminately to indicate not so much the objective character of the interval relationship, but how the listener reacts to it. Obviously the words "good" and "bad" can hardly be applied uncritically to such basic musical materials as tone relationships. Their "goodness" or "badness" depends upon particular contexts within particular musical styles. For example, in the suave and elegant tone world of Palestrina some of the intervals marked D are "bad": that is to say, bad within the aesthetic limits of the Palestrina style. They are not a part of Palestrina's melodic art. He doesn't use them. Isolated appearances of any of these intervals would be startling, out of character with the other elements of his style, and would be heard as faults. The very same intervals appear again and again in Bach's melodies when the composer wishes to create an area of melodic tension, and they sound "natural," "good," and perfectly consistent with the other elements of his style.

From the aesthetic point of view the ears and minds of listener, performer, and composer determine the consonance or dissonance of any interval. From the acoustical point of view, there are objective differences between different intervals. A prevalent theory of dissonance and consonance which dates all the way back to Pythagoras, explains the more consonant intervals as those whose frequencies can be expressed in a simple mathematical ratio. Thus the unison would be 1:1; the octave, 1:2; fifth, 2:3; fourth, 3:4; etc. The interval of the large seventh would be 9:16 and the small seventh 8:15. In the theory the simpler fractions belong to the most static intervals, and the more complex fractions indicate higher interval tension. The main objection to this theory is that even when an interval is sung or played slightly out of tune we still hear it as an octave or a fifth or a seventh with the dissonance-consonance properties of the particular interval, even though the ratio which would be derived from say an octave a few vibrations out of tune would be an enormously large number. Our pianos are even systematically tuned out of tune (tempered) by the piano tuner. The interval of the fifth, which has the Pythagorean ratio 2:3, has approximately the ratio 293/439 in tempered tuning. Yet we are able to hear 293:439 as a relatively static interval!

There are other theories of dissonance, too, all of

them ingenious, but none fully adequate to explain the practice of composers. For our purposes, a complete theoretical-physical explanation is unnecessary, since we are investigating the practice and usage of composers rather than physical laws and principles. Therefore we can define (for musical purposes) the differences between consonant and dissonant melodic intervals in terms of relative tension, using words like static and dynamic to reflect characteristics upon which moderate public agreement may be obtained.

Octaves, perfect fifths, perfect fourths, and, to a lesser degree, thirds and sixths, sound relatively static in most styles. Sevenths and ninths sound relatively dynamic as do most augmented and diminished intervals. These intervals are not absolutely static or dynamic. Even among the "static" intervals, some will prove more "dynamic" than others: in the group of "dynamic" intervals some will sound relatively less "dynamic" and even "static" in some contexts.

In a style such as Palestrina's, which uses only relatively static intervals, small differences in interval tension will have great musical import. So much of his melodic motion is stepwise that *any* skip expresses relative tension, but among the consonances at his disposal, not all express tension to the same degree. For example, Palestrina may use the octave to express strong tension or he may not, but he will always use the minor sixth as a tension interval, even though it is a smaller skip than the octave, and even though it is one of the consonances. When Bach uses the same interval of the sixth, he treats it more often than not as a fairly static interval. Another example: in medieval times the tritone (augmented fourth or diminished fifth) was usually avoided. The prevailing attitude toward it is reflected in its nickname—*diabolus in musica* the devil in music. From about 1600 on it appears with increasing frequency, and in the melodies of a composer such as Schoenberg the tritone is treated as a very low tension interval.

Keeping in mind the fact that the same interval may have different meanings and expressive purposes in various styles, let us see how static and dynamic intervals do their work. We saw, in the familiar Bach theme, how tension was produced on the last note in measure two and the last note of measure three through the use of both tonic and

Fugue in G Major, J. S. Bach

agogic accents: In each case the particular note is higher and longer than its neighbors. Moreover, in each instance the note is approached by an upward skip. All of these tension-producing elements are reinforced by the interval tensions. The high note C, in measure two, is preceded by a D, thus producing the skip of a seventh, a high tension interval. The interval F♯ to E, in the third measure, produces another seventh. The high tension intervals reinforce the tension points of the phrase. The dynamic, rest-seeking skips of the seventh help to create the accent and at the same time urge the melodic line ahead. Bach has used all the means at his command, agogic and tonic accents, a skip up against gravity plus the interval tension itself to make the climax of the phrase musically convincing.

Another extremely beautiful and expressive use of the seventh skip is in Purcell's Four Part Fantasia #4. The energy created by that skip drives the line

Fantasia in Four Parts, Henry Purcell

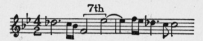

energetically toward the Db after touching first the ornamental high F. Try substituting a G for the F in the first measure; this would alter the interval to a skip of the sixth, a less dynamic interval. See how the phrase suffers without the energetic, tense, forward drive created by the more dissonant skip.

Interval tensions are at work in all melodies, no matter what the style, but in musical styles whose melodies are composed primarily of more consonant intervals, such as that of Palestrina, the intervallic tensions are differentiated so slightly that the modern ear needs training to accept them as real differences. Interval tensions are used freely in the melodies of more recent composers. One example from

MELODY

Krenek's *Lamentatio Jeremiae Prophetae*, must suffice. There is a seventh skip on the first *convertere*,

Lamentations of Jeremiah, for Chorus, Ernst Krenek

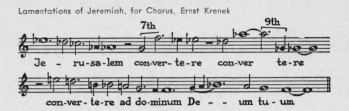

used in much the same way as the seventh skip in the Purcell example. The downward skip from A flat to G flat on the second *convertere* is especially interesting. The skip down creates a certain relaxation because of its direction, but tension is maintained and melodic elasticity guaranteed through the use of a dynamic interval. Thus the composer is able to create a point of rest, far distant from the high note, without in any way causing the line to break or to lose its forward tendency.

HOW MELODIES EXPAND I

Up to this point we have discussed melody from the point of view of the single phrase, and we have concerned ourselves with beginnings rather than continuations. But the single phrases and sentences of a composition are meaningful only as parts of an organic whole. When you write a letter you think in words, phrases, and sentences, and you choose the particular word or phrase with regard for the idea you wish to express. Moreover, in good prose the sentences not only follow one another on the page, but are related in a meaningful way to each other and to your idea. In music there is a similar relation between phrases and sentences. We may be inclined to think that the theme of a composition is somehow the most imaginative part of the music. This is simply not true of contrapuntal music and it is probably not true in other idioms either. Not that themes are unimportant. If the composer has imagination and inventiveness, it will certainly show up in his themes. But the composer's imagination works all the time, in the continuations as well as in the beginnings. The notion that composers are "inspired" with themes is bad enough, but when it is allied in the minds of many musical people with the conviction that the "working out" of themes is a more or less mechanical procedure, an entirely false impression of the nature of musical creativity is formed.

The elaboration and development of thematic material is not less imaginative, not less creative, than the invention of themes. One could even make a fair case for the contrary view: that in many masterpieces the themes are ordinary, or show no special imaginative distinction. Haydn was very fond of using extremely simple themes, even dull ones, in order to build from unprepossessing materials movements of stunning imagination. The opening of the first movement of Beethoven's Fifth Symphony is certainly impressive, but the little figure ...- becomes meaningful, not through any connotation of Fate knocking on the door, nor even because three dots and a dash symbolize the letter V in Morse code or Victory to Mr. Churchill—not for any character which the figure possesses by itself, except the meagre three dots and a dash: three repeated notes, and a skip down a third to a longer note. The meaning of the figure, its importance and significance, comes through what happens to it during the whole ten minutes of music which follows its first statement. The melodic fragments (they can hardly be called themes) which Mozart uses to spin out the glorious finale of his *Jupiter Symphony* are literally tags of melody, stereotypes which were in no sense original or profound creations in themselves.

One of Bach's finest works, the *Musical Offering,* is composed entirely from and upon a theme which he did not even invent. When in 1747 Bach visited the music-loving Frederick the Great, the king, perhaps to test him, gave him a theme and asked him to improvise a fugue from it. Bach not only improvised a creditable fugue, but later wrote a garland of canons of various sorts, a trio sonata and another magnificent six voice fugue, using in each composition the same royal theme. He had this *Musical Offering* engraved at his own expense and sent it to the king. Obviously none of Bach's invention went into the creation of the theme, all his imagination was concentrated on the extremely beautiful and varied elaborations which he drew from it.

The whole art of the chorale prelude, of which Bach was such a master, was to elaborate and reinterpret a melody, one of the chorale tunes of the Lutheran service. A comparison between Bach's chorale preludes and those of his predecessors and contemporaries shows strikingly how rich his melodic imagination was. Too rich for some of the sour parishioners of his church. They registered a formal protest against him on the grounds that he overelaborated the chorale tunes, clothing them in such rich and vivid melodic garments that they were unrecognizable.

I do not mean to imply that themes should lack imagination, far from it. Only very great masters can draw fine music from unprepossessing material. Usually if a composer's themes lack imagination his continuations suffer from the same fault. Themes are crucially important to the composer, not because he concentrates his creative activity only upon them, but for a totally different reason. His judgment of a theme is in terms of its potential—What can be done with it? How can it be varied, developed, combined and elaborated? These questions, so practical, are likely to sound "inartistic" to the person who imagines that the writing of music is entirely a matter of "inspiration." He would make the composer into a musical automaton who merely writes down the cascades of melody which come into his head fully formed—a stenographer to his muse. But composing is an active process. The composer works with a very real, material, sound. It cannot be seen or felt and this quality has much to do with the mystery which surrounds discussions of the composing process. A glance at a composer's working sketches would dispel much of this mystery. Here one can see the tonal material being turned and twisted, scratched out and reformed, until it reaches its final state.

Beethoven's manuscript sketch for part of the *Lenore Overture* #2

The composer's practical attitude toward the theme extends even further. He is often more concerned with the tiny motives which make up the theme than with the theme itself. These melodic fragments are the primary building materials, the bricks and lumber of music. Cell-like they coalesce to form the larger units, the phrases, sentences, and paragraphs of the music. To the listener, they are "sub-microscopic"; like microbes, even when they cannot be seen with the naked eye, their effects can be felt. These effects are of such far-reaching musical importance that it will be well worth-while to study them in detail.

The first part of the familiar theme of the first movement of Mozart's G Minor Symphony contains only two motives, the two eighth notes followed by a quarter note in descending stepwise motion, and the skip of a sixth upward in quarter notes.

The first motive, which is repeated, moved to different pitch positions and even altered intervallically, maintains a certain identity because its rhythm and accent pattern is kept, and because its general pitch contour, stepwise motion downward, is preserved. One would hardly expect so much melody from such restricted resources, and it is indeed a cause for wonder, but when one discovers the extent to which this motive pervades the whole movement, how it unifies and gives continuity, weight and drive, one is amazed! Here is imagination of the highest order, clear and disciplined yet fantastically rich in detail. This is no mere mechanical manipulation of motives. The purpose and function of the motives is clearly to provide the material, the basic stuff from which the music is spun. Yet the motives are not counters to be

Symphony in G Minor, W. A. Mozart

All motives or variants marked "A" are clearly related. The "B" motive is of lesser importance and the segments marked "B?" should most probably be considered as new contrasting elements rather than as transformations of "B", since the only element they have in common is the quarter note motion. It is futile to play the academic game of motive hunting; motive derivations which look well on paper are of little use if they can't be heard. One should be especially careful, in analyzing the music of Mozart and Haydn, to accept only the most obvious motive relationships and derivations, because during the Classical period they usually played only a secondary role in the musical organization.

juggled around until they fall into a melodic pattern. They do not limit Mozart's imagination, they channel it by providing, like grains of dust in the atmosphere, tiny points around which musical ideas may condense.

Themes commonly contain several different motives, but the composer is not obliged to use them all. He may spin out the musical web from motivic fragments which seem at first to be the least important or interesting elements of the theme, or he may use motives which are so obviously identified with the sense and expression of the theme that we hear them as thematic fragments, parts of a cracked up theme, whenever they recur. In the Adagio from his C♯

Minor Quartet, Beethoven uses a theme which splits naturally into two sharply contrasting parts. Later

C# Minor Quartet, Fugue, Beethoven

the first half of the theme appears in such configurations as

© E. F. Kalmus, Inc.

The second half appears in even more transformations, but throughout the composition the basic identity of neither of the motives is lost. The "hearability" of the motive structure is reinforced because the expressive character of each of the motives is consistently maintained. The motive, 🎵 is always active, moving toward tension. Its character is supported by Beethoven's dynamic markings: a quick rise in volume during the first three notes followed by a heavy accent (*sforzando*) immediately released on the note A; then the last part

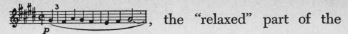, the "relaxed" part of the theme, carrying the marking, *piano*. Throughout the movement, passages which make use of the first motive are associated with sharp rises in volume and movements toward points of climax, and passages based upon the second motive are usually associated with relaxations and lessening of volume. The whole fugue, certainly one of the finest creations a man has ever produced, flowers from the two germinal ideas of the theme, which bud and branch out to amplify and give palpable form to the profound duality expressed by the theme itself.

To scotch at the start any notion that a complete musical analysis can be made by merely bracketing neatly all the motives and their variations, I wish to point out that the melodic materials in measures five, six, and seven assume a great deal of importance in the composition. The motives, from those measures,

, cannot be disregarded

as structural units, but for now we shall limit ourselves to the two main ones.

Of the many devices or techniques which Beethoven uses to create extended melodies, none is more important than sequence: repetition of the motive on a different pitch level. The motive is the second half of the theme, played twice as fast (in eighth notes) as in its original form. The line is a single unit even though it is made up of three repe-

titions of the same melodic motive—a melodic sequence.

Next to bald repetition, this is perhaps the most
common technique in melody writing. Sequences are
especially useful in contrapuntal melodies, where the
melodic movement must be strongly directional in
character, and where tension must be built into the
line itself.

Sequence is really dynamic repetition. A little
experiment will prove the point. Compare these two
melodies:

Notice how different the feeling of motion is in the
two melodies, even though the same motive is used
in both. In the first the motive is simply repeated;
the music moves forward in time, but because the
pitch level of the motive remains unchanged the
music has a static feeling. The forward motion in
time in the second melody is reinforced by the
changes of pitch level which accompany each repetition of the motive, and the line seems to expand

and move more purposefully. To put the matter in other terms, the unity which is guaranteed by the repetition of the motive is vitalized and diversified through pitch changes of the motive.

The sequential process may be seen in detail in the following passage from Beethoven's C♯ Minor Quartet. At the beginning a variation of the first motive is expanded sequentially to create the climactic point of the phrase, and part of the second motive is used in descending sequence as the tension relaxes. Notice how clearly the motive structure shows through the melody, and how the expressive purpose of each of the two motives is expanded and intensified through the use of sequences.

Fugue from C♯ Minor Quartet, Beethoven

Sequence moving up will tend to create climax, but the effect of tension may be enhanced by shortening (cutting) the motive after it has been repeated several times, as in this passage from the middle of the movement. After two repetitions of the motive (this

Fugue from C♯ Minor Quartet, Beethoven

the structure of music

time another variant of the original) Beethoven continues the sequence with only the first three notes as a unit. This shortening of the expected rhythmic unit enhances the forward drive, even though the actual motion is still in eighth notes.

A Melody and its Diminution

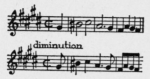

The time values are diminished by ½. ♩ becomes ♪, ♩ becomes ♪, etc.

The eighth note motion indicates another change in the motive. Not only has the technique of shortening been used, but in relation to the original rhythmic values the motive is moving twice as fast, in eighth notes instead of quarter notes. Diminution, the name for this device, creates the effect of hurry simply because of the higher rate of speed. But when thematic or motivic materials are diminished they are not only speeded up but concentrated in time. The whole effect of the passage at the first double bar in the following excerpt—the sudden mysterious yet inevitable change in speed, almost like a temporary loss of balance, a dizziness—depends upon this device; and the sweet, high singing *dolce* which follows owes a great part of its effect to the return to the original rhythmic values of the theme.

The opposite idea, doubling instead of halving the rhythmic values of the motive, is called augmentation. Obviously, if motive diminution can be used to

Fugue from C♯ Minor Quartet, Beethoven

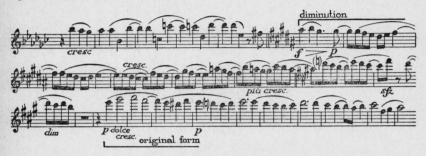

create tension, motive augmentation can be employed to create effects of relaxation and slowing down. In actual practice, motive augmentation is not so common as diminution. I mentioned earlier that the composer's main problem in melody writing is to create convincing points of tension, climaxes; that is perhaps the reason why motive diminution appears so often. Augmentation, whether of theme or motive can be used to create tension too. Beethoven uses it toward the end of the C♯ Minor Quartet Fugue to broaden and give emphasis to a climax. The theme appears in augmentation only once, and the composer does not apply the device systematically to any of the motives. (See example below).

The motivic structure of musical lines is not always so clearly audible as it is in the Beethoven example. Motives may be varied so much that we are hardly

conscious of their original identities, and one might
ask, "If you can't hear them what musical importance

Fugue from C# Minor Quartet, Beethoven

© E. F. Kalmus Inc.

can they possibly have?" When the motive is inverted or played backwards or stretched out of shape
rhythmically, is the composer merely playing private
games, making puzzles, or do such extreme variants
of the motive have some real musical value?

Of course they do. We hear melodic lines as wholes
when we listen to music. We don't say, "Aha! There

is the first motive. There is the diminution of the second motive!" No, we hear the line as a unified organism moving in time toward points of tension and rest. If an utterly foreign motive were introduced into the line at some point, we would hear immediately the lack of fitness, even though as listeners we might not be prepared to say exactly what was wrong. For example, we may not be at all conscious of the motives as such, in the slow movement from the Bach "Second Brandenburg Concerto," but we feel the effects of the motive structure as "rightness" and logi-

Bach Brandenburg Concerto #2, Second Movement

cal order. The order is "unheard" in the sense that we may not be fully conscious of every individual twist and turn of the motive, but if the order were disturbed, even in the smallest way, we would feel the "wrongness" and the lack of order.

Throughout the "Brandenburg Concerto" movement the treatment of the motives is relatively simple, but in the Prelude from his *Sixth English Suite,* Bach inverts and diminishes motives to create variety within the unity of the movement. We accept these motive variants easily, indeed in a movement of this length, if the composer didn't use a good many variants of his motivic material, the composition would probably sound dull and uninteresting. Notice that the motives keep their rhythmic profiles throughout the transformations and variations. The pitch skeleton of a motive may be thoroughly distorted, but if its rhythm is maintained the motive will often keep some sort of identity which the ear will accept.

English Suite #6, Prelude, J. S. Bach

The original form of the melody. Beginning of the movement

Complete inversion of the above melody. Same rhythm.

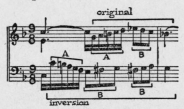

Original form and inverted form appearing together. Slight variation of original form.

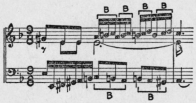

Inversion of "B" motive diminished, appearing with original melody complete. Diminished form in 16th notes in treble clef.

On the other hand, if the pitch skeleton is maintained and the rhythm skeleton is altered, the order thus obtained is more difficult for untrained ears to follow. I don't mean to imply that such an order would be of less value artistically. On the contrary, the variety in detail of constantly changing rhythmic configurations has been exploited, especially by contemporary composers, to create works of great richness. The ideal of "maximum variety from a minimum of means," aimed at by Schoenberg and many of the more recent atonal composers, is reflected again and again in their music: complete rhythmic variation of a very few melodic motives.

Perhaps no single work from this school of composers shows such finesse in its motive structure as the *Concerto for Nine Instruments*, Opus 24, by Anton Webern. Webern is so motive conscious that in his music we can hardly speak of themes! Everything, even the harmony, is motivically derived. In the Finale from the Concerto for Nine Instruments below, the whole expansion, all the music, is drawn from a single motive of only three notes, F♮, F♯, D♮. This is varied in every possible way: it is inverted, played backwards, upside down and backwards. Its intervals are moved into different octave positions, and it is compressed in time to sound simultaneously as a chord.

Here is an entirely different conception of the motive from the one found in the Beethoven Fugue just examined. Beethoven used the motives so that they retained their particular expressive characters throughout the movement, even when they were subjected to variation, but in the Webern piece the

Finale from Concerto for Nine Instruments, Anton Webern

The three-note motive is enclosed by brackets. Notice how much melodic variety the composer draws out of it by transposing it and by changing the octave positions of the notes, even though each appearance of the motive is rigidly separated from the next either by rests or contrasting rhythms.

motive is expressively neutral. It is the rock bottom material of the music. From it contrasting motives with particular expressive purposes are evolved, and these motives (which are really rhythmic variants of the basic motive) form the melodic line. The impression of almost fanatical integrity stems from the fact that every single melodic turn is in some way a variant of a single motive. All the contrasts, sometimes violent and always closely juxtaposed, pulling the music toward a complexity so dense that the mind must summon all its powers simply to follow the sense, are related. Not just related, but variants of a single motivic entity.

Perhaps the reader recoils from the idea of such a

"rational" musical structure. The rigor and precision of the piece *is* a little frightening to the casual music lover. It seems so *planned*, so austere. Its motive organization is not different in kind from that of the Beethoven fugue or the movement of the "Brandenburg Concerto," but it is so complete, so concentrated and so all-inclusive, that, compared with it, the Bach and Beethoven pieces seem to be loosely constructed.

There is, of course, always the danger that a composer will produce melodies which analyze brilliantly but do not sound well. What looks well on paper doesn't always speak to the ear. In my opinion, Webern's melodies are real music. They move, they are alive, they have that tension between unity and diversity (a diversity so ever-changing, kaleidoscopic, like blossoming crystals; a unity absolute—one tiny three-note motive) which one finds only in the finest works. Their classic economy should not lead us to a hasty judgment that the composer is a mere note juggler, even though the lines are difficult to follow. As listeners we would do better to try to grasp and assimilate the immense variety which he gives us. For the variety in the unity is the mark of the music's vitality.

HOW MELODIES EXPAND II

Not all melodies are so "rationally" organized with respect to motive structure. Webern's radical melodic style, which in the above example eschews even themes and concentrates on the complete variation of a single motive, presents an extreme case. Most melodies are much more freely constructed. Even in Bach's music, where the motive structure is quite controlled, there are many passages where the music simply spins out by means of stereotyped musical figures which have no motivic significance. Any attempt to account motivically for every note of a melody is a serious mistake. The analyses of some scholars, which, in order to "account for everything," require the dropping of notes or the adding of notes and various other intellectual strategems which have little relation to the sounding music, leave the impression that the composer was fiendishly clever, and little else. Any melody, even when it has a tight motive structure, is more than a collection of motives and variants. It is an aesthetic whole with a character and mode of action peculiar to itself. Motivic variation, sequence, etc., are only some of the means through which the composer is able to create areas of tension and relaxation on a large scale.

A vast amount of music exists which has little or no dependence upon motivic elaboration. To us, reared on the music of Bach, Beethoven, Haydn, Brahms, etc., the logic, even the musicality, of such melodies might be hard to conceive. But a melody without sharply profiled motives, without sequences, without a clearly articulated phrase structure, can be just as beautiful as the most "rationally" organized melody by Bach or Beethoven.

the structure of music

Consider the following melody by Okeghem, from his *Missa Prolationem,* a melody almost absolutely different in its conception from those of Webern, Bach and Beethoven.

Sanctus (opening) from Missa Prolationem, Okeghem

Tension points, indicated with asterisks, are irregularly spaced. Notice in the top voice how the notes C D E, ornamented and unornamented, shift their rhythmic pattern at each climax point. See too how the motion becomes intensified toward the end of the section through the use of ♩ and ♪ notes.

There are no clearly audible motives, no sequences; there is no breaking of the line into easily grasped units. Smoothly, the musical present grows directly out of the immediate past. The gentle, unbroken, almost amorphous flow undulates, swells and ebbs, yet pushes irresistibly ahead toward its future, a cadential goal far distant from the phrase's beginning.

Continuity is everything, the all-encompassing ideal. That is the reason why everything which might interrupt the flow—sharply profiled motives, rests between parts of phrases, repetition, sequence—is banished. The logic of the melody is hardly "rational" in the Bach or Webern sense, because all the usual structural elements of melody are missing. Yet the melody "makes sense." The wavelike motions toward high notes, the pushing and ebbing which somehow grows organically to a climax, have a mysterious rightness.

These climax points, the points of melodic tension, are the key to Okeghem's melodic style. The spacing of the high points, their relation to each other and to the highest point of the phrase, articulates and organizes the melodic stream without impeding its forward progress. The means used to express the tension and relaxation are extremely limited—stepwise motion, a few melodic skips and a small variety of note values. From these few elements the composer makes the most subtly differentiated climaxes, the finest gradations of accent.

The indescribably rich effect of his melodies is in great part due to the bubbling vitality with which the ever new is evolved from the old. Never is there any repetition in the ordinary sense; instead a luxurious growth of melodic forms. However, the always new is so slightly different from the old that in spite of the ceaseless variety one hears a unity. A unity of continuity, always new but always the same, like a silkworm's thread.

Okeghem's melodic style may be more easily understood seen against the whole background of Medieval and Renaissance music. In the very earliest kinds of polyphony composers used a borrowed melody, usually a Gregorian chant, to provide the structural basis for the composition. Above and below this *cantus firmus,* i.e., "fixed song," the composer wrote new lines to accompany and to decorate it. He conceived his melodies as ornaments to the fixed song. The *cantus firmus* provided the "rational" element, releasing the invented melodies so that they could expand in a free and even improvisatory way. By the fifteenth century the techniques of *cantus firmus* writing were so highly developed that a single *cantus firmus* was able to provide the "rational" structure for a whole mass. Quite a few were on a grand scale, larger in dimension and longer than many 19th century symphonies! One of the earliest *cantus firmus* masses, on the tune, *Alma Redemptoris Mater,* is by Leonel Power, an Englishman. Here is an excerpt from the *Sanctus* which shows the typical non-sequential, freely unfolding, ornamental style of the times.

Alma Redemptoris Mater (Gregorian Chant)

The section of the above Gregorian chant which is used in the *in nomine* section below is enclosed with dotted lines. The chant appears completely in every section of the Ordinary of the Leonel mass.

Okeghem wrote many *cantus firmus* masses too, developing the style to a high refinement. This ex-

R. D. Lawrence Feininger's edition of Leonel Power's *Alma Redemptoris Mater* as printed in the Documenta Polyphoniae Liturgicae Sanctae Ecclesiae Romanae published by the Societas Universalis Sanctae Ceciliae.
© Carl Fisher, Inc.

The Gregorian version of the chant is placed on the small staff below the music to show how a rhythmicised version of a chant suitable for use as a *cantus firmus,* is created. Even visually it is obvious how the invented melody winds around and adorns the chant.

> cerpt from his *L'Homme Armé* mass shows the orna-mental-decorative melodic line and its dependence upon a *cantus firmus* in an especially clear fashion.

Agnus Dei III from Missa L'Homme Armé, Okeghem

© Harvard University Press

This is not the only method which medieval composers used to create a "rational" structure for extended compositions. They decorated and ornamented the borrowed melodies themselves, treating them in a manner analogous to that of the jazz musician improvising on a well-known theme. Both medieval composer and jazz improviser often change the tune radically, even to the extent of making it almost unrecognizable. Both may hide it, refer to it obliquely, or use it merely as the taking off point for their newly created melodies. Yet the borrowed melody provides the "rational" element. It is the only stable thing in the swirling melodic flux.

Here is part of a *Kyrie* by Binchois, a contemporary of Dufay, in which the top voice is an ornamented and rhythmicized version of the Gregorian *Kyrie, "Cunctipotens Genitor."*

Kyrie for Three Voices, Gilles Binchois

© Musikhaus Klavierbauer Bessler, Goslar, Germany

The asterisks mark the tones of the third section of the Gregorian *Kyrie, Cunctipotens Genitor.* Although the notes are from the chant, the rhythm and the added cadential formulas change its character completely. The two bottom voices are not related thematically or motivically to the top voice. They are of secondary importance melodically, and were probably not sung but performed instrumentally.

Sometimes the melodic ornamentation of an existing melody was combined with other *cantus firmus* techniques to make an extremely dense yet flexible melodic unity. This is what Dufay does in one of his most beautiful masses, "*Se Le Face Pale.*" The tune, a familiar one in his day, is a secular love song. It appears as a *cantus firmus* in every section of the Ordinary of the mass and in decorated and ornamented forms in the other voices as well. Sometimes the melodies have an obvious relation to the tune, but often they refer to it only vaguely. The tune does not provide motivic materials for melodic expansion, as do themes, subjects and borrowed materials in the music of Bach, Mozart, Beethoven and later composers. You do not even hear the complete tune as a tune anywhere in the mass. It is so covered up with a twiney network of melodic garlands that it loses its corporeality and becomes almost an abstraction. Yet everywhere the special fragrance of "*Se Le Face*" breathes out of the melodies like a perfume.

In the excerpt from the *Credo,* notice how at the opening the tune appears at once in two different ornamented versions. On just this one page there are three versions of "*Se Le Face*": the tune itself, used as a *cantus firmus;* the voice on the middle staff, an ornamented version of the first part of the tune; and the top voice, an ornamented version of the middle voice! When the *cantus firmus* enters, the other voices drop the tune and proceed with independent melodic lines.

Now one can catch a glimmer of the "rationale" of

Okeghem's "irrational" type of melody. The melodies of his *Sanctus* are similar in character to those which he ordinarily wrote to *cantus firmi*: they are non-motivic, non-sequential, freely asymmetrical in phrase and accent pattern. But in this composition he left out the fixed song! The melodies therefore have no common point of reference, no pillar around which to twine. They are related directly. Instead of the fixed and somewhat static relation of melody decorating borrowed material, the composer has his free unbounded melodic threads braced only against each other in a constantly changing balance of forces.

Interest in melodic designs which do not involve motivic or thematic elaboration has been revived by some contemporary composers. Alois Haba has developed the notion of an athematic style most consistently, but the tendency toward athematicism may also be observed in the works of Schoenberg, and surprisingly (in the light of the motive treatment in his *Concerto for Nine Instruments*) in many of Webern's compositions. Many of Schoenberg's compositions, especially those written between 1910 and 1920, are very free, motivically and thematically.

In later compositions he has used the twelve tone technique as the structural basis of a composition in such a way that the tone row is treated as the "given," rather than as a fixed motive or collection of motives. The tone row then provides an organizing force simply because it is always there: the new is always the old in a new guise, even though sharply profiled motives, repetitions, etc., are dispensed with. The perfume of the tone row permeates the composition even when the row itself cannot be easily recognized. Like a *cantus firmus* it does not need to be "heard" in order to perform its structural functions.

Music written along these lines is difficult to understand for the same reasons as Okeghem's, especially when no rhythmic profile is maintained throughout numerous variations of the tone row or tone row segment. Significantly, the most successful athematic compositions by Webern and Schoenberg are vocal or program music. The text or program provides the skeleton, the "rational" element, allowing the composer almost complete melodic freedom. In their instrumental music, especially in contrapuntal textures, both composers consistently use a more rigorous kind of motive treatment.

HARMONY

I pointed out earlier that all polyphonic music has horizontal and vertical aspects, two dimensions, represented by melody and chord. When two or more melodies are written to sound together, chords are formed. If the music is well written, the chords and melodies will sound as though they belong to each other. Neither will have been written at the expense of the other. Melody and harmony will complement each other in the large as well as the small details of the music.

Therefore, it is quite unrealistic to try to separate music into a study of melody and harmony. Harmonic implications are in every melodic figure, even the smallest motive, and melody is involved in every progression from one chord to another. I have separated the two elements to simplify the discussion, but toward the end of this chapter I will try to show some of the ways in which melody and harmony interact with each other.

At cadence points, those "sensitive" areas in the musical organization, the effects of the harmony, and the character of the relationships between melody and chord are most easy to grasp. The tone of relaxation or relative rest in the melody is supported by a chord of rest in the harmony. These resting places are of varying degrees of finality; some cadences are even more like hesitations, momentary stopping points. Nevertheless, all are places of lower tension and relative relaxation; for that reason they have some connotation of finality.

Language has a variety of cadences, too. At the end of a sentence, the voice falls; to express a question, we use a rising inflection. We have evolved written symbols, commas, periods, semicolons, question marks, etc., to designate these inflections, in order to articulate both spoken and written words. The analogy between such inflections and cadences is quite precise and may help us here.

Take the matter of finality. How does one make a sentence end? One stops for a moment, of course, but often the voice drops melodically, too, to a rather undefined lower pitch. This lower pitch, though variable from sentence to sentence, depending upon meaning, intensity of emotion, etc., is an area of relative rest.

In music, the pitch of the tones of relaxation can

be accurately located. The composer is able to use one particular tone as a final or tonic, composing the music in such a way that at points of tension the chosen tonic or final does not appear and at points of rest it does. Moreover, he may construct a chord which reinforces and expresses this tonic so that when he desires the effect of finality he has at his disposal both a tonic tone and a tonic chord.

It is not the final tone by itself which makes for the feeling of finality, but its relation to the other musical tones. The composer creates melodic configurations, contexts of tones, in order to make the final actually sound final. The sentence does not end because of the period—the period is there because the sentence has ended. Similarly, in chordal relationships the final chord of a cadence, the chord of rest, can only be made to sound final if it is placed in certain relationships with other chords.

The special melodic and harmonic configurations that are cadences are more or less stylized musical patterns, owing their effectiveness in part to common cultural acceptance. Styles in cadences change fairly fast; they must because they constantly tend to become mere formulas. Composers, striving like writers, for precise personal expression, change the language as they use it. Cadences which we accept as giving a satisfying feeling of finality would sound bewildering and perhaps completely meaningless to people living only forty or fifty years ago; conversely, we often discover that we need to make a special effort to understand the cadences of medieval composers.

Here is a cadence common during the fifteenth

century. Its strangeness will help us to understand how cadences function, because we will take nothing for granted, as might be the case with a cadence from a more familiar musical style.

Soprano
Alto

Tenor
Bass

The melodic cadential effect is concentrated in the upper line, especially in the melody of the last two measures. The figure is the nub. It appears and reappears in music from the fourteenth through the sixteenth centuries, and was thoroughly familiar to musicians and listeners. It creates the effect of finality by beginning on the final, moving downward one-half step to what was later to be called the "leading-tone" (because the tone has such an inexorable tendency to move toward the final or tonic). Then it moves downward one more tone before skipping back to the final note of rest. Even the rhythmic character of the figure is involved in creating the finality: the faster notes make a rhythmic tension which is resolved at the final note.

Harmonically the finality is created through a progression of chords, that is to say, a patterned relationship between a series of chords. The final chord is built on the bass tone G; both top voice and bottom voice sound the tone of rest—G. The chords preceding it are all built from the bass note D. If we separate the vertical progressions in the next to the

the structure of music

last measure, we note that each quarter note of the melodic figure has a different vertical configuration. There are four different chords, each with the bottom note D.

The movement from the D in the bass to the G in the bass expresses the harmonic sense of the passage —the movement from chords built on the tone a perfect fifth above the final to the chord built on the final. (In the example the actual movement is a perfect fourth up in the bass, but harmonically D up to G is equal to D down to G.) Harmonic tension is resolved by moving from a chord not the tonic chord to the tonic chord itself.

Which is more essential to the feeling of finality, the harmony or the melody? The question is impossible to answer definitely. Each voice, not only the top one, moves melodically to help create the finality: top voice to the tonic, bottom voice to the tonic, tenor voice to the tonic. Only the alto voice goes to a tone other than the tonic, filling out the chord. Nevertheless, the voices moving purposefully create harmonies which have their own effectiveness. We shall come back to the question of this interaction between chord and melody again, but for the moment the cadence as a whole musical organism must claim our attention.

The great power of the cadence to articulate musical speech is shown in a striking way in the following chanson by Guillaume Dufay, *"Adieu m'-*

Adieu m'amour, Guillaume Dufay

Cadences are written in larger notes. Notice that in addition to having a cadence in the harmonic and melodic sense, each phrase is set off from the next by rests.

amour." Each melodic unit is bounded and finished off by a cadence of some sort. Moreover, there is always a rest before the melody begins again. In this short composition there are six strong cadences, and more than any other single element in the music, they give it the qualities of clarity and balance. By framing the phrases the cadences cut the music into easily assimilable sections, and because the cadences are related to each other in a logical manner, they also act to unify the whole composition.

The pattern of relationships between cadences expresses specifically harmonic relationships between the phrases. The first phrase cadences on F; since nothing heard up to this point challenges that cadence we accept the tone F as a home base. The ear and musical mind does this easily and without especially thinking about it. The second phrase cadences on D and the third on C. Now if you play over that much of the composition you will find that even though the cadence on C is a strong one, the music does not seem to want to end there. Musical sensibility demands a return to the home base for a complete sense of finality. That complete finality does not come until the composer wants to end the composition. Then there is a cadence on F. But notice that the first cadence on F in the last line is not permitted to come to a complete stop, rhythmically; the composer bridges it with melodic motion in the accompanying voices. The concluding phrase, also cadencing on F, clinches the return to home base.

The pattern of the cadences is strictly harmonic in

conception, and this short composition, using as it does the notion of a home base to which each cadence is related, is an early example of tonality.

TONALITY

The principle of tonality is not at all complicated. It rests upon the notion of a home base. This base is the place of rest, expressed either by a single tone or by a chord built upon that tone. Phrases in the Dufay piece which cadence upon the home tone are heard as belonging to its tonal area. Phrases which cadence upon other tones are in areas of tension; from the harmonic point of view, away from home base. Thus the same principle which dominated the discussion of melody is here in the harmonic sphere too: tension and relaxation, the ebb and swell of chords in patterned relationships.

Only the cadence areas express clear harmonic relationships in Dufay's composition. The harmonic effects of cadences are localized and the home base feeling is by no means the dominating structural principle. But later when tonality became more completely developed, it became one of the most important structural principles in Western music, providing the bricks and beams for the grand designs of the composers of the seventeenth, eighteenth and nineteenth centuries.

The most important chord in tonal music is the triad. It is composed of three different tones (hence the name, triad); not any three different tones, but three tones, each of which is the distance of a third from its neighbor.

Triads

Diatonic Scale

A Triad on the 5th Degree

There are four different types of triads, as illustrated above. Each tone of a diatonic scale has its own triad (when you sing the scale of do, re, mi, fa, sol, la, ti, do, you are singing a diatonic scale) and we may speak of a triad having the tonic as its root as a "triad on the first degree," or one built upon the fifth degree of the scale, "a triad on the fifth degree," etc. The scale degrees are usually indicated by Roman numerals in musical analysis.

Triads of the Scale of C Major

The relationships between these seven triads provide the fundamental chordal materials of tonal music. Some relations are of course more important than others. One, the relation between the tonic triad and the triad on the fifth degree, dominates all others.

The simple harmonic contrast which was exploited in the cadences of early modal music, that is to say, the contrast between a triad on the final and almost any other triad, gave way to a thoroughly organized system of harmonic relationships. The pattern of harmonic contrast changed slowly from I—"any other" to I-V. Then the fifth relation was extended to chords other than I and V. Triads on II and VI are a fifth apart, as are those on III and VII, and IV and I. (From IV to I is a fifth up.) If all the triads are put in fifth relations and strung out as a progression a rather satisfying little sequence of chords results: I-IV (a fifth down) IV-VII (a fifth down) VII-III (a fifth down) III-VI (a fifth down) VI-II (a fifth down) II-V (a fifth down) and V-I. See below.

These fourths upward are equal to the fifth movement downward. The line could not move down in fifths continuously, as the staff is not large enough

le structure of music

to contain the movement. Each triad in this progression of chords, the harmonic underpinning of many a passage of tonal music, is in a fifth relation to the one following it. Fifth relations permeate the whole progression from beginning to end.

The importance to tonality of chords lying a fifth apart can be demonstrated even more simply. Three chords, triads on I, IV, and V, are enough to express a key in the simplest way. The V chord lies a fifth above the tonic and the IV chord a fifth below.

Both chords converge upon the tonic. The movement IV to I is parallel to the movement V to I: IV-I is a rising, V-I is a falling fifth. Composers during the seventeenth, eighteenth, and nineteenth centuries used these three chords in many stereotyped forms for final cadences, and the progression IV-V-I came to be known as an authentic cadence. They meant by authentic, the cadence which has most "final feeling."

We have already seen how a cadence creates a point of rest. Now if cadential ideas are extended to cover the whole chordal aspect of the composition we can easily understand how the above progression could, by dominating the piece, create the feeling of, not merely a cadential point of rest, but a point of rest so powerful that it could become a home base. Tonal composers extrapolated large structures from the simple movement I-IV-V-I. A whole first section of a composition might be harmonically related to the I area; a contrasting section could be built around the area of IV or V; then a final section, perhaps even a repetition of the first section, would return to the I area, the home base, in order to round off the composition. Symphonies, operas, all the great classical forms used these principles. The sonata-allegro form, the grand formal idea of the classicists, was not essentially a matter of themes at all, but of key areas. And patterned key areas are nothing more than chord progressions expanded in time.

Keys are entirely harmonic structures. They do not pre-exist. They are constructed by the composer when he uses chords in particular sequences to express a particular key. This feeling of "keyishness" is one in which we are at all times aware in one way or another of "where we are in relation to home." We place ourselves harmonically, we orient ourselves in the music, by relating our position to the tonic. A key gives unity to all the musical events which happen in it in much the same way that linear perspective organizes all the picture space in relation to a single point. In perspective, the spatial events are related to each other, given position, depth, etc., by means of a vanishing point. In a key, the tonic, the home base, is analogous to the vanishing point. It provides the focal point to which every musical event is bound, the unifying point through which all the musical events are related to one another.

The stability of a particular key, its "keyishness," the pulling power of its home base, can be controlled by the composer. He may loosen or tighten the key feeling at will. He may even move smoothly or abruptly from one key to another, a process known as modulation. To effect a modulation he customarily relies on the harmonic ambiguity of a chord or a group of chords. Any triad can be interpreted as belonging to several keys, depending upon the chords which precede and follow it. A chord may be approached in the key of C major, then reinterpreted and followed by chords belonging to F major. Context makes all the difference in meaning. The single chord on which the modulation pivots is tonally ambiguous in the same way that the spoken words "would" and "wood" are ambiguous until placed in a context of other words.

TONALITY THEN AND NOW

The great forming power of tonality rests on these simple ideas: (1) a home base; (2) harmonic movement to areas within a key or even to new keys, in order to express harmonic tension, which (3) is finally resolved by a return to the home base. The stability of the home base, the harmonic distances covered, even the means used to effect them, have varied enormously between 1600 and the present day; in general, the harmonic language has tended toward increasing complexity. During the past century the tendency accelerated to a headlong run, and during the past forty years changes have moved at a gallop.

While its explorers probed Africa and the Amazon, and its painters searched for new and exotic color relationships, the composers of the late nineteenth century expanded their keys. They looked for new relationships between chords and for new chords which expressed the traditional relationships in fresh ways. An impetuous urge toward intense emotional expression sparked the hunt.

Seventh Chords in C Major

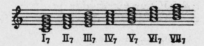

I₇   II₇   III₇   IV₇   V₇   VI₇   VII₇

Triads were dressed up and intensified in various ways, although the essential root relations between them were retained almost to the end of the century. Seventh chords on all scale degrees, ninth chords, even eleventh and thirteenth chords on the fifth degree, became more common. These high intensity chords gave their music a new—and to those who first heard it, a shocking—character. It sounded revolutionary, cacophonous, and to some ears appeared to be the very antithesis of tonal music.

It was different, but so far as tonality was concerned, not revolutionary. As long as the root relation between V and I is maintained, it matters little

Ninth Chord on 5th Degree, C Major

to the sense of "keyishness" whether or not the V chord is a triad or a ninth chord. The costume of the chord has been changed, it may be clothed in shiny new, or bold and clashing colors, but so long as the chord is some kind of V chord moving to some kind of a I chord, the essential harmonic relationship will sound. That the chords of the seventh, ninth, elev-

Eleventh & Thirteenth Chords

enth, and thirteenth are powerful dissonances makes not the slightest difference to the feeling of "keyishness."

But other chords which composers used more and more extensively *did* affect the stability of the key in a roundabout way. They are called altered chords.

In order to explain the meaning of the word, altered, we must examine the distinction between diatonic and chromatic. When you sing do, re mi, fa, sol, la, ti, do, you have a diatonic scale. All of the familiar major and minor scales are diatonic, and were derived from the medieval modal scales. These scales are really patterned sequences of whole and half steps. In the common do, re, mi, fa, sol, la, ti, do scale, there are half steps between mi-fa and ti-do. All the other intervals are whole steps.

Now imagine a scale from "do" to "do" (or C to C) in which every interval is a half step. This is a chromatic scale.

C Major

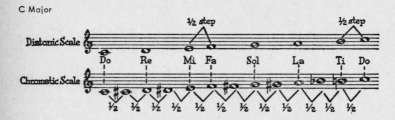

Every altered chord has one or more of its tones changed chromatically. The color of such a chord

C Major

changes radically, because the interior relations between the intervals making up the chord have been disturbed from the diatonic norm.

If the two versions of the same progression given above are compared, it will be discovered that even more is involved musically than a change of color in the IV chord. The IV chord with the chromatic alteration (the second version) leads more strongly toward the V chord than the unaltered IV chord. The tendency of the A flat toward the G is much more powerful than the A toward the G. We are back to melody again! The pull of the A flat toward the G is a melodic, not a harmonic motion.

Half step motions, tendency tones seeking points of relative rest, may be understood as extensions of the leading tone principle. In a key, melodic motion to the home base is most convincing when it progresses from the leading tone to the tonic. The leading tone is the seventh degree of the scale. You will get some idea of its tendency toward the tonic tone if you sing do, re, mi, fa, sol, la, ti—leaving out the final "do." The "ti" tends toward "do," and to some persons the sense of "keyishness" implicit in the scale is so strong that they feel physically uncomfortable if it is left incomplete.

Composers expanded the leading tone principle by tonicizing scale tones other than the tonic. Any tone needing a special emphasis conceivably could have a "leading tone," a tendency tone, placed before it. Moreover, the upward driving leading tone was complemented by another which has a downward tendency. In the following progression, the chord of the augmented sixth, that sounds so dear to lovers of barber shop harmony, includes both types of tendency tones.

Tendency tones appear in great profusion in the music of Wagner and his contemporaries, to the point of clogging the harmonic flow. The chords change so often that the music must necessarily be slow moving, otherwise the chord changes would go by so fast that they couldn't be grasped.

C Major

The two G's in the final chord are the tones needing the emphasis. In the top voice F#-G and in the bottom voice A♭-G, are the tendency tones. The chord itself may be thought of as a "tendency chord," since its whole function is to emphasize the V chord.

There are so many altered chords and so much of the melodic motion is chromatic in Wagner's latest works, that the essential root relations which guarantee the "keyishness" are almost completely obscured. This is especially true of his opera, *Tristan and Isolde,* where melodic considerations and highly colored chords dominate the music to such an extent that for long periods any clear feeling of a stable key is completely lost. The following excerpt illustrates this chromaticization of the harmony. True, it could be analyzed from the point of view of root relationships, but such an analysis would have little congruence with the musical sense. The harmony is more expressive than structural, and melodic motions affect the harmonic life at every turn.

Wagner's kind of tonality, with its emphasis on

harmonic ambiguity, tonal expansion, chord color and chord intensity, mirrors his aesthetic goals, boundlessness, continuous expansion, emotionalism.

Tristan and Isolde, Act II, Wagner

© G. Schirmer, Inc.

Arrows indicate tendency tones. Notice how the bass moves almost entirely with chromatic motion, further obscuring the sense of root movements. The melodic motion of the other lines is equally chromatic, and there are few unaltered chords to be found.

He turned the emphasis in tonality from the simple root relations between triads representing scale degrees to a continuously modulated, ambiguously fluctuating stream of varicolored chords. He thought chordally to such an extent that many other musical elements in his style are almost atrophied, but as a harmonist he was such a genius that he, more than any other single man, laid the foundations for later harmonic developments, neo-modality, atonality and the like.

Reacting to Wagner and some of the more suffocating aspects of his music, many composers retreated from the chromatic type of tonality and sought a simpler sort. This style has been called neo-modal or pan-diatonic, though neither term describes it very well. Characteristically, it is diatonic and relies upon fairly stable key areas, at least in comparison to Wagner. Music written in this style often foregoes or heavily masks the dominant and subdominant functions, those fundamental root relations which order the older tonal music. Because the dominant and subdominant functions are weakened or missing, the label neo-modal has been attached.

But the music of Stravinsky, and he is supposed to write within that general idiom, can hardly be described by either of these terms. His kind of tonality is certainly different from Wagner's—it is selective, exclusive, diatonic; and modal elements may be found in it along with many other things—but whenever the feeling of "keyishness" is present, when there is a home base, no matter how different in musical effect from the music of Wagner or Mozart, his music is tonal. We are apt to want to save the word tonality for some particular period or style. This is a mistake, and merely obscures the meaning of the word. Dufay's tonality is certainly different from Bach's; Bach's is different from Beethoven's,

Beethoven's from Schubert's; Stravinsky's and Bartok's from Wagner's, but all of them use the basic principle of tonality.

Another group of contemporary composers has accepted the chromaticization of music and has attempted to use the whole chromatic gamut in its compositions without relying on any of the traditional harmonic-chordal functions. Atonality, the word applied to this style, is another misnomer. Pan-tonality would be a better word, for all possible relations between tones are used in creating the music. The word atonality is, however, fairly well established, and is useful for making rough distinctions between styles which rely heavily on the traditional means of tonality and those which do not. But an absolute distinction between tonality and atonality proves faulty, because in a large proportion of atonal music, tonal "areas" (not keys of course) are established and motion to and from these areas takes place. These tensions and relaxations are, however, not tied to a harmonic-chordal base or bass. Root relations between chords do not make the essential vertical structure; rather, the melodic and harmonic elements are so involved with each other and so interdependent that so far as the musical event is concerned, harmony and melody are twin facets of a single thing.

Right now, when we are in the midst of atonality, hardly acquainted with a notion only forty years old, it is impossible to venture an "explanation" of it, much less to abstract and codify its "harmony." We feel movements from place to place; composers are able to control them, and listeners to hear them. Leave it to some future theorist to look back: he may even find that the style which we now call atonal is yet another kind of tonality.

One thing is certain: all modern harmonic idioms are more melody centered than chord centered. Linear relationships, melodic relationships, have a significance and an importance to the over-all musical structure which has been missing from music for over a hundred years. Chords, in the wide sense of vertical relationships, are as important as they were in the past, but now they are approached much more from the melodic-linear point of view. New means for creating vertical tension are being exploited, means which reflect the contrapuntal nature of much contemporary music.

DISSONANCE-CONSONANCE

Some of the new means involve the use of hitherto unheard of dissonances. But music has never been without dissonances, especially linear music, which can hardly get along without them. From its very beginnings, contrapuntal music has exploited the vertical tensions generated by the clash of voices, and the systole and diastole of dissonance and resolution.

What is a dissonance? Not an easy question, for many reasons. Philosophers, and more recently scientists, have worked on the problem for over a thousand years, and no satisfactory physical theory completely congruent to musical practice has yet been found. We discussed the Pythagorean theory—that consonances were musical expressions of simple arithmetical ratios, dissonances complex ratios—in an earlier chapter. A summary of some later investigations may help us to understand dissonance and consonance more fully, insofar as they function in music.

Helmholtz advanced two theories in his famous book, *Sensations of Tone*: the theory of beats and the theory of *Klangverwandschaft* (tone relationship). In the theory of beats a pair of tones is considered consonant when no disturbing beats are heard. Beats are produced when the acoustical phenomenon known as interference takes place. The "interference" is between two sound waves differing in pitch. Vibrating simultaneously, they produce minute intensifications many times a second. If the intensifications (beats) number less than six or more than 120 per second they are least disturbing, and pairs of tones falling within these limits (more than 120, less than 6 beats per second) would be considered consonant. All interval relations, except the unison, produce beats, but the consonances have beat patterns which are tolerable to the ear. For example, the roughness due to beats heard in the interval of the fifth is not so harsh as the roughness of a seventh.

The theory has only one serious fault, that the number of beats produced by any interval varies from octave to octave. This would make it appear that the consonance or dissonance of an interval changes according to whether it is played in a high or a low octave. Helmholtz draws attention to the fact that certain intervals sound more harsh when they are played in the deep pitch ranges; he cites the well known fact that thirds, which sound well in medium or high range, tend to sound muddy in the bass. He also mentions that composers have always composed with regard for such differences between high and low range. What he says is perfectly true as far as it goes, but the fact remains that unless the difference is between a very high or a very low range, music is heard and composed in such a way that the intervals are equal and interchangeable from octave to octave.

Helmholtz emphasized that from the physical point of view no absolute distinction can be made between consonance and dissonance. Rather there is a gradation between "most consonant" and "most dissonant." But during his lifetime composers continued to use dissonances as though there *were* such a distinction and theorists tended to regard consonance and dissonance as opposite states. Perhaps in order to account for current music theory, he developed the *Klangverwandschaft* theory. In this way he was able to make a clear distinction between dissonance and consonance. Two tones were defined as consonant whenever their harmonics (overtones) had tones in common. Helmholtz had to exclude the seventh and ninth harmonics in order to make the theory work. For that reason it is not so convincing as the theory of beats, although its distinctions between consonances and dissonances are well in accord with the practice of tonal music up until the end of the nineteenth century.

More recently consonance and dissonance have been investigated fruitfully from a psychological and statistical viewpoint. Stumpf's *Tonverschmelzung* (fusion) theory relies upon the ability of the human ear and mind to fuse or separate tones. He defines dissonances as those pairs of tones which are most often heard as two separate tones when sounded together. Consonances are those in which the two tones are most often heard as fused into one. His theory makes no sharp distinction between consonances and dissonances; it merely ranks pairs of intervals in order from very consonant to very dissonant. Including the observer and his judgments, it frankly accepts the subjective aspects of the problem.

The fact that no sharp distinction can be made here between consonance and dissonance may be helpful. Although we may have to accept a certain blurring of terms, a different point of view should help us to see the problem afresh. Older theories have been interpreted in such a way that consonance was made equal to concord and pleasure; dissonance to discord and pain. Dissonance and ugliness were associated. One more step and it became possible to say, "all dissonances are ugly, all consonances are beautiful," although all the music of the ages refutes such a rash notion. Yet, because "dissonances are ugly," a false and almost meaningless statement, the fiction that no "good" music used dissonances had to be maintained, and aesthetic discussions acquired fervent moralistic overtones. Even today the word dissonance is like a red rag to some musical doctrinaires.

The real meaning of dissonance in music is not discord, ugliness, but tension—tension in relation to other more relaxed intervals. Every theory we have mentioned supports this interpretation, even though the details—which intervals are tense and which relaxed —may vary a great deal from one style to another.

Consonance and dissonance *may* be treated as opposite states. This is true of the Palestrina style and more generally of the whole of Renaissance and Medieval music. But from about the middle of the nineteenth century to the present day dissonance has come to be handled more and more as relative to consonance. Contemporary music does not throw the idea of consonance out the window, but instead of two absolutely opposing states, consonant and dissonant, it substitutes the notion of graduated dissonances, from very weak to very strong.

Dissonance should be thought of as a positive force rather than an unavoidable or ugly necessity. It performs many functions in counterpoint, not the least of which is in promoting the linearity of the music. Stumpf's theory rested on the assumption that the more dissonant intervals resisted fusion; they tended to be heard as separated tones. Certainly lines which are dissonant to each other will stay apart and lines consonant to each other at every point will be more likely to fuse into a homogeneous sound. Of course, it is not enough to "use plenty of dissonances"—they must be used properly. The problem is to keep the lines separate without making a cacaphony, to create that delicate balance between vertical and horizontal tensions, without which the music would sound lifeless and dull.

The ebb and flow of consonance and dissonance helps to create the contour of the phrase, it reinforces cadence points, it is of primary importance in climaxes, it helps to articulate the sections and members of a composition. It functions at every level of the music, even below the phrase, where it helps create the accentual tensions and relaxations from within.

If dissonance is a state of tension, the tones comprising the dissonance are necessarily active. They seek places of relative relaxation, and therefore have characteristics of melodic tendency somewhat analogous to the tendency tones discussed above. But whereas tendency tones get their drive from the attraction of a tonic, temporary or real, and have for that reason a tendency in a particular direction, the tones of a dissonance tend only "ahead." The tension state will be succeeded by relaxation, but the individual voices may move in a variety of ways: upward, downward, by skip upward, or by skip downward. The dissonance propels the individual voices ahead, and in doing so supports the drive of the individual melodic lines. The lines in turn move in such a way that vertical patterns, alternating between states of tension and relaxation, ensue.

The intervals accepted and used as consonant and dissonant vary considerably from style to style and even from composer to composer. In the eleventh century the perfect fourth was a consonance and thirds were dissonances. By the fourteenth century fourths were dissonances and thirds were consonances. Sevenths and ninths, which fifty or sixty years ago were used exclusively as high tension intervals, now are heard in low tension, consonant combinations.

The acoustical fact that some intervals have more tension than others does not bind composers to use them in particular ways. The important thing in any style is that *for this music,* even *for this particular composition,* there are hearable differences between various vertical tensions. In some contemporary compositions the lowest level of dissonance—the areas of relaxation and rest—is represented by what would be considered high tension chords in Palestrina's time. But nowadays our ears easily accept seventh and ninth chords, symmetrical fourth chords and other combinations as places of relative rest, *so long as they are in relation to other chords of higher tension.* A level of relaxation has to be established and kept in relation to areas of tension. The relation is essential, even though it may take many musical forms. The triad may be the low tension combination, the consonant "norm," as it is in the music of Bach, Haydn, Beethoven, etc.; or seventh chords may function that way—see many passages from Wagner, Debussy, contemporary jazz, etc.; or the level of lowest tension may be so low that the triad is considered a high tension chord. This situation exists in some early

medieval music, where final chords are always uni
sons, octaves or perfect fifths.

Resolutions of Dissonances

The musical process of moving from vertical tension to vertical relaxation is called resolution. When
each of the voices making up a dissonance moves in
such a way that the following vertical sound is of
lesser tension and in obvious relation to the dissonance, the dissonance is said to be resolved.

Not all dissonances need resolution, only the obvious ones. But what does "obvious" mean? The
"obvious" places in the musical texture are the accented notes, and dissonances which appear at these
points are usually treated differently than those
which are on unaccented beats. For example, in
4/4 time there are four quarter note beats in every
measure. The time signature implies (exceptions in
contemporary music were discussed in the chapter on
melody) that the first beat and the third beat are
normally accented. Now dissonances on the first and
third quarter notes have a very different musical effect from dissonances on the second and fourth beats.
Dissonances on the unaccented or weak beats are un-
obtrusive so long as the melodic motion is stepwise.
They sound as though they were merely connecting
the tones which appear on the accented first and

third beats. For this reason dissonances such as these, on weak beats, connecting two other tones by means of stepwise motion, are called passing dissonances or passing tones.

The dissonances which appear on strong beats are the ones which need resolution. They attract attention because of their metrical position. The tension created by the coincidence of accent and dissonance needs to be relaxed somehow. Musical practice varies tremendously from style to style, but, for the present, let us discuss some more or less typical resolutions for the sake of grasping the principle involved.

Appoggiaturas (Downward)

Appoggiaturas (Upward)

Here is a dissonance-consonance pattern in which the top voice does the resolving. The E moves stepwise downward to the D, the other voice repeats the

F; then the top voice moves downward from the C to B and the lower voice holds the D. Such resolutions stepwise downward are very common, because the relaxation in vertical tension is supported by the downward relaxing melodic motion. Resolutions upward are not quite so convincing because they lack this melodic help, but may be heard in music from most historical periods. Patterns such as these, where the dissonance is on the accented beat and resolved through stepwise motion on the following beat, are called appoggiaturas.

The other important type of strong beat dissonance, the suspension, is nothing more than a modified appoggiatura. The appoggiatura's effect—coming down hard on the dissonance, then resolving—is strong and uncompromising. In a suspension the path through the dissonance is smoothed. The dissonance is "prepared" as well as resolved. If we prepare an appoggiatura it will look and sound like this:

If this suspension is compared with two other similar consonance-dissonance patterns, its special character may be seen easily.

Suspension (as above)

Suspension (Without Tie)

Appoggiatura

The top example has the suspension. The next lower example has a suspension without the tie, ⌢. If these two are compared it will be found that it is the tying over of the tone from the preceding consonance which smooths out the strong beat dissonance. The bottom example has the same dissonance-consonance pattern, but the upper voice approaches the dissonance in such a way that an appoggiatura is formed.

It may be difficult for a reader without special musical skills to follow what seems to him excessively fine differences between dissonances on strong beats, dissonances on weak beats, stepwise motion, preparation and all the rest. Nevertheless, dissonance treatment is of primary importance to musical structure, and he should have some notion of how it operates. A simple presentation of the workings of consonance and dissonance in music of two different styles should, at the very least, demonstrate how necessary vertical tensions and relaxations are to music, and how varied the ways in which they are used.

Within the general framework of tonality, Bach uses dissonances to support melodic tensions and relaxations. The devices just explained, suspension, passing tone, appoggiatura, are very much in evidence, and contribute to the musical drive. See the dissonant pile-up in the first score of the following excerpt from Bach's *Art of Fugue*, and how it is released at the final measure of that score. And the

Art of Fugue Contrapunctus #4, J. S. Bach

Dissonances are marked with an X. Suspensions are marked (X) and appoggiaturas [X].

striking build up of tension throughout the last five measures.

The passage below from Paul Hindemith's Fourth Quartet, apparently so different, uses a much wider range of dissonance tension, all the way from thirds, fourths, fifths, sixths (and triads in the portions where several voices take part), to extremely dissonant combinations. Although simple suspensions, appoggiaturas and passing tones are rather rare, there are many appoggiatura and suspension types, expansions of the older forms. Resolutions of appoggiaturas and suspensions tend to be from strong dissonances to weaker dissonances. Tensions are built up over longer periods of time, rather than dissonating and resolving from accent to accent. The climax creating effect of a gradual build up of dissonance is exceptionally clear. Notice how consonant the opening, and how smooth the growth and release of vertical tension.

Composers have recently begun to use the dissonance texture itself, instead of key relationships, modulations, etc., to articulate the large musical design. A section with relatively weak dissonances may be contrasted with another containing much stronger dissonances. With new means comes an awareness of new formal possibilities. A graduated scale of disso-

Quartet #4, Paul Hindemith

Lines connect notes which are dissonant to each other.

nances can create a climax just as surely (more surely
in a contrapuntal style) as a pattern of root and key
relationships, although the shape and character of

such a climax will necessarily be different from a climax achieved through the means of tonality. Similarly, sections can be contrasted just as sharply through a controlled use of dissonance contrast as through change of key, modulation or any of the other tonal devices.

Such structure, emerging entirely from the lines and their relationships, has a certain advantage over a counterpoint which is bound to a harmonic-chordal conception. This does not mean, of course, that good counterpoint cannot be written within the tonal system; Bach's music alone would refute such a notion. But it is important to understand that the dissonant character of so much of our significant contemporary music, far from being evidence of weakness or decadence, is the true sign of its linear integrity.

INTERRELATIONSHIP BETWEEN CHORD AND LINE

Throughout the chapters on harmony and melody, I have tried to emphasize the opposition between linear ideas and chordal ideas. But the obvious differences between a line and a chord could easily tempt us to conceive of them as living absolutely independent existences in the music.

Heard music is a whole, not a beautiful assortment of tones or intervals or rhythms, or melodies or harmonies, but a complex unity, alive with a variety of tensions and relaxations, some taking place in the vertical, some in the horizontal, dimension. When we abstract only the melodic element, or only the harmonic element, we necessarily take a partial view, and, so long as we remain conscious of what we are about, it can lead us to many insights.

However, such partial views may also lead to the "nothing but" fallacies:—"Harmonies are nothing but the places where the lines meet," or its inversion, "Melodies are nothing but the surface of a chord progression." The separate tones of any chord in a musical context have melodic tendencies. The chord may be likened to a tightly clutched handful of watchsprings, where every tone, though for the moment held stationary, is full of melodic potential.

On the other hand, every time a melody skips it creates harmonic implications. The melodic interval has a harmonic effect which may be extremely important to the sense of the music. There are harmonic implications in every cadence, too, and the pattern of cadences and climax points may be part of a large-scale harmonic plan.

Melodies *are* sometimes hardly more than chords strung out in time, and chords *are* sometimes merely collections of tones, but more often there is a web of interrelation, and a rich interplay between melody and chord. They influence each other, they are involved with each other and share each other's destinies.

COUNTERPOINT

Imitation is so universal a contrapuntal process that in some textbooks it is equated with counterpoint itself. It appears in every fugue and in almost every symphony; now and then in opera, arrangements of popular songs, and in singing commercials. As the name suggests, one voice repeats the melody of another; a soprano voice may start a melody; when it has progressed a bit an alto voice may start to sing the same melody, while the soprano voice continues its line. The two lines are "on the diagonal" to each other—repetitions are staggered from line to line. This shows up clearly in the excerpt from Orlando di Lasso's little two part motet, *"Justus Cor Suum*

Justus Cor Suum Tradet, Orlando di Lasso

Tradet." The two almost identical parts, leader and follower, are, from beginning to end, related to each other by means of imitation.

Imitation is actually a very ancient idea. It is used in some of the earliest Western polyphony, the organa of the twelfth and thirteenth centuries, and from the fifteenth century on, it has been the most important contrapuntal procedure. And Curt Sachs has pointed out in his book, *The Rise of Music in the Ancient World,* how primitive peoples spontaneously improvise in imitative style, and he speculates that imitation may have originally grown out of the practice of antiphonal singing. In answering back and forth, one group usually waits for the other to finish; but

Imitation from Malacca   (After Sachs)

COUNTERPOINT

if some of the singers, under the stress of emotion, should begin the tune before the rest have finished, the tune would overlap itself.

Whatever its origins, the reason that imitation is such an important musical process is because it is, like sequence, a form of repetition. Now repetition is the simplest type of musical extension. Used properly it can be a most satisfying musical device, but if unrelieved it can also become, like the drip, drip, drip of a leaky faucet, excruciatingly boring. We need repetition for the unity it makes, but we also need to have variety within the unity. Sequence, the repetition of a melodic figure or motive on different pitch levels, is such a valuable device simply because the need for unity is served, while sufficient contrast is

Gradual Justus ut Palma, Heinrich Isaac

Each voice entrance begins on D. All the voices except the bass imitate exactly and hold to the imitation for a few measures. The melody is slightly varied in the bass voice, but its identity is hardly disturbed.

provided by pitch changes to keep the melodic line from sounding dull. The kinship between sequence-repetition and imitation is very close, because imitation is nothing but repetition distributed throughout several voices. Here are two short illustrative examples. In the first, the repetition is exact; there is no change of pitch when the motive is repeated.

In the following example the repetition takes place on different pitch levels, a sequence-like procedure.

Fugue in D Major, Well-Tempered Clavier, J. S. Bach

Imitations are on different pitch levels, A, E and B. The sequential effect is intensified here because the melody itself is sequential—the motive is enclosed in the bracket—thus doubling the overall sequence effect.

The repetitions weaving through all the voices bind the parts together to produce a unity of texture. All the music is woven of the same kind of thread, and while the ear may never be able to follow every detail of each separate melodic line, it has no difficulty in comprehending such textures as those illustrated above as musical wholes.

Memory and recognition play some part in the perception of such a unity. The melodic motives which move from voice to voice need to be recognizable and differentiated from one another, otherwise the ear will not be able to separate and distinguish them. If the imitating voice answers with the inversion or diminution or augmentation of the leading voice, then obviously the total effect will lose some of the character of repetition or sequence, because the ear and mind will have to grasp more complex relationships. If the distance of the imitation is very small so that repetitions are squashed together, or if the distance of the imitation is very large, the repetition-sequence effect may be quite obscured. Nevertheless, such varied imitations do have a unifying effect. Even when they are extremely complex and beyond easy following, we are able to feel this "unheard" order.

Imitative textures are unified wholes, but if the melodic ideas are themselves completely undifferentiated, the whole is liable to be a unified blur, vapid and featureless. There is plenty of this sort of counterpoint about, gelatinous stuff which excites in the listener only pity for the composer who expended so much labor upon it. More than anything else such academic manipulations of musical material have given counterpoint a bad name among music lovers.

The "Fantasias" of Henry Purcell are anything but academic and featureless. The whole tradition of Elizabethan madrigal and fancy writing sings through these pieces which he wrote at the very beginning of his career. But there is something bold and new about them too. Purcell was not merely looking over his shoulder at a precious past. The past was in him, and firmly in it he pushed toward new and unexplored ideas. Ideas so new at times that today we hear his music with that shock which comes when we recognize our own. Here is a short passage from his "Fantasia in Four Parts, #6," written on June 23rd, 1680, when he was only 22 years old.

Fantasia in Four Parts #6, Henry Purcell

The melodic content of the passage consists of the three fragments marked 1, 2, and 3. They are moved from voice to voice, and are placed in different contexts at each appearance. Sometimes they are varied slightly; 3 is inverted several times, and at one point 1 and 2 are inverted. The whole warp and woof of the music is woven from these three melodic strands. The texture which emerges seems extremely complex, but if we pinpoint one melodic fragment at a time and follow its wanderings, we can easily see how large a role is played by repetition.

In the following diagram the pattern of repetition for the first motive only is illustrated.

Here is the pattern for the second motive.

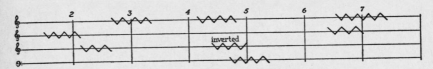

The third motive is not repeated so many times, perhaps because it is more complex. It may be also that Purcell wanted to save it for the climax of the sentence, where it appears twice in close imitation, measures 5 and 6.

If we now superimpose all three of these repetition patterns, some notion of the quality of the texture may be visualized.

This is, of course, only a very rough approximation of the musical texture. Viewed vertically, the four voices make a melody in depth—see especially measures 1 and 2, and measure 5, where all three motives are superimposed. At any point in the music, at least two motives are sounded simultaneously. This makes for a strong feeling of unity, which is, however, infused with movement and variety, because the three different melodic motives always appear in new contexts.

Faced with such subtle art, one is startled to discover that the three melodic fragments are not mere melodic counters which the composer moved mechanically from voice to voice. Compare the melodies of the soprano and tenor parts and see how different they are, even though they use the same 1, 2, 3, succession of motives.

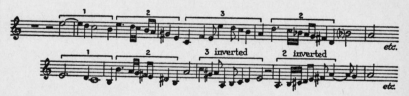

They are two entirely disparate melodies, yet they are related, like brother and sister, through their common parentage. The various motives which make them up are not merely juxtaposed, but grown together; two different ways of growing have produced two different things.

Here is a living realization of the unmechanical, almost biological connection, between part and whole in music. The melodic fragments are real parts; they can be recognized and they have definite personalities, yet they continually recoalesce to form higher melodic unities and the even larger heard unity, that dense fabric of meaning in which the animation of the parts serves only to illuminate the sense of the whole.

COMPLEMENTARY RHYTHM AND ACCENT

Keeping in mind the analogy between contrapuntal textures and woven fabrics, imagine for a moment the wide variety of materials which may be woven on a single loom. Some are of such a fine weave that one needs a magnifying glass to distinguish the individual threads. Others, perhaps woven more loosely, or from different colored materials, or different types of fibres, metal or cellophane, are more obviously linear. Neither in woven fabrics, nor in music, can one make absolute distinctions between weaves which are homogeneous and weaves which are not. Two textiles, one woven 100 threads to the inch, and the other 50 to the inch, could both be homogeneous in texture, and obviously a textile woven 2 threads to the inch would be less homogeneous than another woven 100 to the inch. There is an almost infinite gradation of possible textures, and it would be futile to try to set up rules and regulations to determine at what point a texture stops sounding linear and takes on homogeneous qualities.

Imitative textures in music may be homogeneous or not, depending upon the desire of the composer, the general style in which he is writing, and other factors. Imitation does not in itself guarantee that the music will sound linear in the ear. For example, the beginning of the madrigal by Andrea Gabrieli, *"Ecco l'aurora con l'aurata fronte,"* (Lo, how Aurora with

Ecco l'Aurora, Andrea Gabrieli

Imitations of the whole melody are bracketed, even when they are not entirely strict. Note that there are also incomplete repetitions, and that both alto and tenor repeat the melody. Both of these things buttress the homogeneous character of the passage.

her golden graces) is solidly imitative, yet it is fairly homogeneous in sound.

There is a certain homogeneity to the melodic texture because the melody is extremely short, simple, and repeated in full no less than seven times. Fragmentary repetitions bolster the unity of the web also. But the passage is homogeneous in a strictly vertical sense. This is because all the important accents, in all of the voices, reinforce each other. The different voices may be singing different things, but there are no real conflicts between accents. The melody is constructed in such a way that the first quarter note of each measure receives a strong accent and the second quarter an almost equally strong one, so, no matter how the entrances of the theme are staggered, first beats of all measures are stressed. And there are no suspensions or other devices used which might deflect the attention from the steady alternation of strong and weak beats. In spite of the fact that the rhythms of the various voices are more or less complementary to each other (one voice holds a note while another moves with faster notes), the prevailing effect is a vertical-chordal one, at least as soon as the third voice has entered.

It is difficult to determine the degree to which the homogeneity is affected by the thickness of the texture—certainly a five part texture has "more threads to the inch" than a two part one—but this particular example would have a homogeneous sound even if it had four voices, instead of five.

The di Lasso piece below, even though it has only

two voices, has inner qualities which make for linearity. The rhythms of the two voices complement each other as in the Gabrieli composition. However, there is more rhythmic variety: Gabrieli used only two different kinds of notes, quarter notes and eighth notes; di Lasso uses whole notes, half notes, quarter notes, eighth notes, dotted quarter notes, and dotted half notes to make the lines stand apart.

Justus Cor Suum Tradet, di Lasso

Reproduced by permission of the copyright owner, Mercury Music Corp.

Compare the following rhythmic diagrams of the di Lasso and Gabrieli excerpts and you will see how di Lasso has opposed patterns of long and short notes to make the melodies move over independently.

Diagram of Rhythm Pattern, Justus Cor, di Lasso

Diagram of Rhythm Pattern, Ecco l'Aurora, Gabrieli

Notice that the overall accent pattern of the Gabrieli madrigal is extremely regular. In measures 7 and 8 when the top two voices enter on the second instead of the first quarter note of the measure, there is a slight intensification of the accentual tension, but the overall effect is regular, and the accents in the various voices hardly contradict each other.

No such uniformity is to be found in di Lasso's composition. Strong accents do not coincide in all of the parts *all* of the time. Sometimes the accents of the individual voices conflict with each other, that is, one voice has a strong, the other a weak accent simultaneously—see measures 8, 9, and 10. Throughout these three measures there is an obvious tightening of the accent pattern. At the beginning of the piece the accents are spaced fairly regularly, but from measure seven the accents come at shorter and irregularly spaced intervals. This concentration of accent, like faster and more labored breathing, together with the tension produced from the conflicting accents of the separate parts, greatly enhances the drive to the climax which comes finally on the first note of measure nine.

The wiry vitality of the Purcell excerpt depends in part upon the same sort of conflicting accents. Moreover, the conflict is often intensified by means of dissonance between the parts. The first two measures, analyzed below, are really quite astonishing.

In any counterpoint the melodies must complement each other, but while di Lasso, Gabrieli and Purcell have all made use of complementary rhythms between the voices, di Lasso and Purcell have used in addition the powerful effects of complementary and conflicting accents between the parts. The composers

Fantasia in Four Parts #6, Purcell

Every tone has been given a melodic accent. The boxes refer to the accent situation in the four parts directy above them. A parenthesis around an accent means that a note is being held at that point; a dash means that the part is resting. Notice how independently the voices move, and how the dissonances are involved with and support the melodic accents.

used conflicting accents to help keep the lines independent and clearly audible as lines; and they controlled the distribution of the accents, concentrating them at tension points, using fewer of them in areas of relative relaxation. The difference between the di Lasso and Purcell and the Gabrieli piece is incalculable. Although all three are imitative textures, di Lasso's and Purcell's music is far more linear in effect.

I do not wish to imply that di Lasso and Purcell have written better music simply because theirs is more linear. The linearity or homogeneity of a piece can hardly serve as an aesthetic category for judgement. Some styles sound homogeneous, some do not. Some are extremely pure and thin in texture and some are thick and heavy. We may be attracted to one type of texture more than to another, but we should resist the temptation to elevate our personal or cultural taste into the realm of objective validity.

Likewise, the strictness of the imitation, or its freedom, cannot be made to serve as a yardstick for aesthetic judgement. Imitation may be strict, in which case it is called canon, or it may be very free, amounting to little more than repetition of phrase beginnings. Both the Purcell and di Lasso excerpts—the Gabrieli too—are examples of free imitation, a term which simply means that the repetitions from voice to voice are varied slightly.

In di Lasso's motet, the imitation is strict as to rhythm but somewhat free melodically. The rhythm of the two voices is identical right up until the last measure, where it is broken in order to form a typical suspension cadence. But the melody of the first voice is changed slightly when it is imitated.

The bottom voice begins its imitation at the interval of an octave—the first voice begins on high D and the second voice on low D—but in measure 4 the interval of the imitation shifts to the fifth below for a few notes. From the end of the 8th measure the lower voice has a quite different melodic skeleton. In measures 10 and 11 both voices must serve the harmonic cadence—imitation is a secondary considera-

Justus Cor, di Lasso

tion for the moment. The two similar melodic lines are close enough in character for us to accept them as "the same thing." But they are not identical, and that is why we call this process free imitation.

In comparison to the excerpt from the Purcell "Fantasia" the di Lasso piece is fairly strict. It is strict as to rhythm, fairly strict melodically, and it is continuously imitative. Di Lasso imitates whole melodic lines, Purcell imitates melodic segments. Purcell makes no effort toward continuous imitation, therefore his imitative textures are of an entirely different sort from di Lasso's. Purcell works for a motivic density which is the very opposite of di Lasso's art, which depends upon a balanced flow of interlocking non-motivic lines.

Less continuous even than Purcell's, is Mozart's use of imitation from his C Major String Quartet, K 465.

Most of the time only two of the four voices are involved in the imitation, and the imitation itself is between melodic fragments rather than between continuous lines of melody. The easily recognizable melodic fragments are tossed back and forth from voice to voice conversationally to create strong repetition-sequence effects. This sort of imitation is very properly called dialogue style. Mozart learned it from Haydn, who first mastered the classical balance between polyphony and homophony in his *Russian Quartets*. Not until Mozart and Haydn had learned to infuse the old "galant" style with counterpoint did the style which we associate with them come of age. Their mature counterpoint is nothing like that of Purcell or Bach, and it has even less in common with the kind of continuous imitation which we find in the works of di Lasso and his contemporaries, but imitation is there, adapted to a different expressive and aesthetic climate.

FUGUE

In Fugue, we may see imitative processes at work on a grand scale, for the very essence of fugue lies in the continuous expansion of a single subject by means of imitation and a few other contrapuntal procedures. Many musical forms and types are essentially imita-

First Movement, Quartet in C Major, K 465, W. A. Mozart

125   COUNTERPOINT

tive—canzona, variation ricercar, motet, madrigal, fantasia, to name a few—but fugue is distinguished from all these by the fact that it is based on a single theme or subject.

A fugue begins with the (usually unaccompanied) announcement of the subject. The voice which first announces the subject then continues its melodic line, while each of the other voices participating in the fugue takes up the subject in turn. When the subject has appeared once in each voice, the music continues to expand by means of sequence and motivic elaboration in all the voices. Areas in the music where the subject appears at least once in each voice are called expositions, whether they appear at the beginning, middle or end of the fugue. The passages of sequential and motivic expansion between expositions are called episodes.

Following is a schematic diagram and the music for the first exposition and the first episode of the Fugue in A Minor from Bach's *Well-Tempered Clavier*.

Note that there is no musical break between exposition and episode below; one flows smoothly into the other. The episode provides variety and relief from the subject, but it grows out of the exposition organically, and the contrast which it makes is in no sense in opposition to the exposition.

Notice that the first time the subject is answered the imitation is not exact. A skip of a third is answered by a step. Fugues in which answers are not identical are called tonal fugues to distinguish them from real fugues where the subject is imitated identically. The distinction is a purely technical one— a tonal fugue is neither better nor worse than a real fugue. The word tonal, used in this connection does not refer to the system of tonality. A tonal fugue could be written within the harmonic idiom of atonality, or a tonal fugue could be entirely in a modal idiom.

The subject of any fugue is made in such a way that the melodic continuations flow easily from it. Its "openendedness" allows for many different continuations. In the example above, each voice begins with the subject but continues quite differently, spinning out a new melodic line, different from, but related motivically, to each of the others.

Sometimes the melodic continuations which follow the subject are so strongly defined, and are used so systematically throughout the composition, that they become almost like independent themes. Then they are called countersubjects. The fugue quoted above has an independent countersubject, marked in the diagram, which provides much of the material for the episodes.

Although a fugue may have a countersubject or even two or three of them, one should not think of such a fugue as having two or more real themes. Countersubjects are usually used as contrast materials. They complement the subject and provide musical variety, but in comparison to the subject, they almost always are of secondary importance.

THE FUGUE AS A WHOLE

The structure at large of a fugue is a series of expositions and episodes. There may be many of them or only a few. They may be long or short; the episodes may be long, the expositions short, or the opposite situation may prevail. The character and distribution of the episodes and expositions, and the pattern they make, will determine the over-all shape of the music, so no two fugues are ever exactly alike in structure. Therefore, the fugue diagrammed below can hardly be taken as a model. Yet it shows in outline how one fugue happens, and insofar as it indicates clearly marked episodes and expositions, it illustrates typical fugal procedure.

Contrapunctus III, Art of Fugue, J. S. Bach

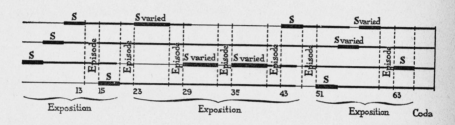

While no fugue can get along without at least one exposition, the first, expositions may appear in many forms. Usually the first exposition is the most "regular." In the fugue diagrammed above, the first exposition has the subject once in each voice, but in the second exposition there is no announcement of the subject in the bottom voice. Moreover, throughout the second exposition the subject appears in a variant form. The wider spacing of subject entries in the middle of the fugue allows for more melodic variety and more contrast of tonal area and key, and it is fairly typical of Bach's procedure.

The subject enters at closer intervals toward the end of the fugue, adding to the musical intensity and supporting the final climax. Two of the entries, those in the top two voices, are slightly overlapped, adding substantially to the feeling of concentration.

For effects of intense concentration and climax, the entries of the subject are often squashed together quite radically, the imitations occurring long before the original announcement is completed. This device, by no means a requirement of every fugue, is called stretto, an Italian word meaning pressed or narrow. Here is a stretto passage which appears toward the end of the D Major fugue from Bach's *Well-Tempered Clavier*. For convenience in reading the four voices are placed on separate staves.

Fugue in D Major, Well-Tempered Clavier, J. S. Bach

Episodes are just as varied in length and character as expositions. Some fugues seem to be all subject, with the episodes little more than breathing places between expositions, while others have extremely long, almost independent episodes. There are some fugues, and even a few by Bach, in which the melodic materials of the episodes are not motivically related to the subject, but these are a small minority. Most episodes are expansions of one or more motives of the subject or countersubject. As a matter of fact, subjects and countersubjects are usually constructed with a view to their possibilities in terms of motivic expansion.

The over-all structure of any fugue is a matter of episodes and expositions balanced and related in such a way that they make a coherent, unified and interesting whole. Every fugue that is well made has a form, a particular shape, but no two fugues are alike, and in no sense can one think of a preexisting "fugue form" into which all fugues can somehow be fitted. The form happens; it is a result of procedures, not a box into which the music is poured, and the form of the fugue, meaning its sensible shape and character, grows out of the musical materials, the subject, countersubject, melodic extensions, etc., and the ways in which that material expands through episode and exposition.

The one thing that all fugues have in common is the quality of continuous expansion, usually, but not always, of a single subject. The melodic materials introduced at the very beginning grow and grow. It is as though one were blowing up a balloon—when the balloon bursts, and when the fugue has reached its maximum expansion, everything is over. This is an entirely different conception of form than we find in the classical sonata, the dance forms, or the romantic symphonic poem. There is nothing rigid or set about it at all, because fugue is a matter not of form but of procedure; it is a way of happening, a process.

This idea of continuous expansion of a single subject is pursued to the uttermost in Bach's last (unfinished) work, *The Art of Fugue*. The composition consists of a group of fugues and canons demonstrating all the principal types and devices of fugue. Every fugue and canon is built from the same theme or a variant of it, and the work as a whole may be considered a gigantic series of contrapuntal variations on the following theme:

Subject of The Art of Fugue, J. S. Bach

© E. F. Kalmus

A short synopsis will help to show the grand dimensions of the music which Bach spun out from this tiny germ. An extended discussion of *The Art of Fugue* is far beyond the scope of this book, and the reader is referred to the excellent *A Companion to the Art of Fugue*, by Donald Tovey, which contains a humane and readable analysis.

The first four contrapuncti are fugues without any devices such as augmentation, diminution or stretto, and are therefore called simple fugues. Contrapuncti I and II are built on the original form of the theme and III and IV on its inversion.

Contrapunctus I and II

Simple fugues on the original theme

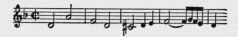

Contrapunctus III and Contrapunctus IV

Simple fugues on the inversion of the theme

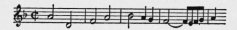

Contrapuncti V through VII are stretto fugues in which the subject appears in combination with its augmented, diminished and inverted forms.

Contrapunctus V

Subject answered by inversion. Entries of the subject overlap (stretto) and the stretto becomes narrower and narrower.

Contrapunctus VI

Subject in direct and inverted forms and in diminution of direct and inverted forms. Almost continuous stretto.

Subject

Answer

Contrapunctus VII

Subject in three different time schemes: original, diminished and augmented. All three in both direct and inverted forms.

Contrapuncti VIII, IX, X and XI, whose themes are shown below, are double or triple fugues (fugues having more than one subject) which use all the resources of double and triple counterpoint. The principles of double and triple counterpoint are discussed at length in the chapter, Interchangeable Counterpoint.

Contrapunctus VIII

A triple fugue, i.e., three different fugues with different subjects joined together to form a whole. In this fugue there is first a complete fugue built upon the first subject appearing below; then the second subject below is introduced in combination with the first subject. Finally the third subject, *The Art of Fugue* theme, enters. After an exposition of its own it is combined with the other two subjects.

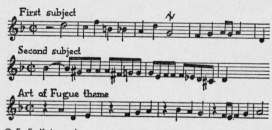

Contrapunctus IX

A double fugue using the following two subjects.

Another double fugue with strettos and complex double counterpoint

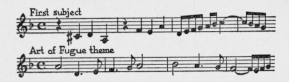

Contrapunctus XI

Another triple fugue, a counterpart to Contrapunctus VIII. It uses the same subjects as Contrapunctus VIII but inverted and in a different order. Toward the end of the fugue, *The Art of Fugue* theme appears simultaneously in its direct and inverted forms.

Contrapuncti XII through XV are two voice canons. Some of them are discussed in the chapter, Canon. And Contrapuncti XVI and XVII are completely invertible fugues, discussed at the end of the chapter, Interchangeable Counterpoint.

Contrapunctus XIX below is the crown of the work. Bach did not live to complete it, but probably planned to make it a quadruple fugue. Of the three subjects, one is based upon the composer's name—in German, the letter H stands for B natural and the letter B for B flat, hence Bach's name would be spelled in music by the notes, B flat, A, C, B natural.

Contrapunctus XIX

© E. F. Kalmus, Inc.

No other single work demonstrates the potentialities of fugal procedures and the individuality and variety possible in fugue as completely as this. *The Art of Fugue* is like a dictionary or an encyclopedia. It is a magnificent compendium for the student, and Bach certainly intended it to be used in that way.

Yet it has a more than didactic purpose. If anything can be called pure music, this is it. Written in open score, there is no hint as to what instrument, or instruments, it was written for. It has been sung, arranged for keyboard, string quartet, and orchestra, and some people have even maintained that it was never meant to be played but only read. Whether materialized through the medium of keyboard, orchestra, or voice, the music will retain its essence so long as the lines can be heard clearly. It is independent of the sound of any particular instrument.

This monumental collection of contrapuntal variations on a single theme, so vast in dimensions and so dense and intricate in detail, is by no means easy to fathom. It requires time and effort and it does not yield up its beauties easily. However, listeners, especially the listeners of this century, must have found their efforts rewarded, for *The Art of Fugue* has come to be accepted by both professional and amateur as one of Bach's greatest, and perhaps his greatest instrumental composition.

FUGUES SINCE BACH

Since fugue is a procedure rather than a form or an idiom, its use is not confined to the Baroque period of music. But Bach's fugues have been accepted as such excellent models that, ever since his time, fugue writing has been heavily influenced by him. He set the style and character of fugue to such an extent that many people are inclined to think uncritically that the only kind of fugue which "really sounds like a fugue" is one written by the patriarch himself.

Both Mozart and (later) Beethoven were influenced by Bach's fugues, partly through the offices of the Baron van Swieten, at whose Sunday morning musicales they heard and performed *The Well-Tempered Clavier* as well as transcriptions of some of the organ fugues. Mozart never became a thoroughgoing, nor ever an entirely successful fugue writer, but Beethoven, who knew and studied many works by both Handel and Bach, adapted fugue to his highly individualized and dramatic style.

Many of Beethoven's late works contain fugues, and with few exceptions they are very different in character from those of either Bach or Handel. They are longer, often with extended episodes and wider ranging modulations, and they are always highly dramatic. The fugue from the *Hammerklavier Sonata*, Opus 107, has a driving intensity and a dramatic character not to be found anywhere in Bach's or Handel's work; and the "Grand Fugue" Opus 130, originally intended as the finale for the B Flat Major Quartet, goes back to sources which antedate Bach. It is a variation fugue, more kin to the early sixteenth and seventeenth century canzonas and ricercars, than to Bach's prevailingly monothematic conceptions.

Haydn, Mozart, and Beethoven all adapted fugal procedures to symphonic and chamber music style through the liberal use of *fugato*. A *fugato* is a passage, sometimes short, sometimes long, where a subject is given a single exposition and then continued freely without the alternation of episodes and expositions to be found in an extended fugue. Beethoven used *fugato* so much in his later symphonies and chamber works that it is almost a mark of his style.

Both Schumann and Brahms wrote fugues which were modeled more along the lines of the Bach fugue. Brahms was especially drawn to the procedure and used it in several of his most popular compositions.

Perhaps in reaction to the anti-structural aesthetic notions which accompanied the final paroxysms of musical romanticism, contemporary composers have shown a new interest in fugal procedures, some modeling their compositions on the Bach fugue and others striking out into new musical territory. Hindemith's *Ludos Tonalis* is a sort of modern day compendium of fugue, although it is marred by a certain heavy-handedness in the melody writing. Bartok has written many fugues and fugatos, the finest of which is the opening movement of his *Music for Strings, Percussion and Celeste*.

Bartok and Hindemith both work within the bounds of a weak tonic type of tonality, but fugue is perfectly adaptable to an atonal idiom too. The finale of Anton Webern's *Concerto for Nine Instruments* on page 58 is fugue-like, and Arnold Schoenberg has used fugal procedures extensively. Alban Berg is adept at *fugatos* of all types and has even introduced a fugue (with the singer taking one of the lines!) into his opera, *Wozzeck*. None of these compositions "sounds like a Bach fugue" of course; the composers use fugal procedures, imitation, exposition, and episode in new ways and in a new idiom, for new expressive purposes.

Ernst Krenek has written a remarkable quadruple fugue for the finale of his Sixth String Quartet which can serve as an excellent illustration of what contemporary composers are about when they use fugue.

The four themes come from earlier movements of

the composition, one from each movement. Then in the final fugue they are combined in a new unity which consummates the whole composition. Classical ideas of formal construction are completely reversed; the complete statement of all the themes of the work comes only at the very end of the composition in the quadruple fugue instead of at the beginning of the work, but from a musical and expressive point of view, the idea is perfectly reasonable. The formal plan simply mirrors the profound difference in outlook between composers of the eighteenth and composers of the twentieth century.

Although it is dangerous to speculate upon what music is about, it seems quite certain that the form of this quartet is intended to reinforce the composer's meaning or expressive intent. He first presents us (in the earlier movements) with four separate aspects of experience which are very different, even antithetical. When we are firmly impressed by the sense of antithesis, he welds these disparate experiences into a new and higher unity which we thought impossible. The quadruple fugue which is the vehicle for the composer's thought is not an exercise or mere demonstration of superior skill, but the essential means for expressing a musical idea.

Canon is the strictest form of imitation. The imitating voice follows the leader exactly, with none of the deviations or slight adjustments which are customary in free imitation. As in imitation, the follower may imitate at any time distance and any pitch interval.

It takes at least two voices to make a canon, but there is no upper limit to the number of voices. Canons in six and eight voices are fairly common, and at least one having forty-eight voices has been composed, but most have from two to five parts.

The composition by Bach which follows below is a four voice canon, completely strict, at the time interval of a half-measure. Moreover, it is a perpetual or circle canon, in construction exactly like a round. The music can go on and on until the singers want to stop, because the end is dovetailed with the beginning.

Canon (Perpetual) for Four Voices, J. S. Bach (from the Bach Reader, H. David and A. Mendel)

Each voice imitates the preceding voice but begins a fifth higher: the first voice begins on C, the second on G, the third on D, the fourth on A. Thus each melody is identical to the leader but on a different pitch level. Note the dovetailing toward the end of the canon, which makes the end fit into the beginning to produce a perpetual or circle canon.

Compared to free imitation, canon is a rigorous procedure, and from time to time it has been criticized on the grounds that it is "unnatural"—so much effort and planning must go into the writing of a canon that the musical result must therefore be highly "artificial." Writers about music sometimes refer to canons disparagingly as "mere puzzles," with the implication that they are incapable of carrying real musical values.

Canonic procedures have been especially maligned by those who hold the notion that composing is a matter of pure inspiration. Naturally, anyone who thinks that music drops into a composer's head out of the clear blue sky, and that all the composer has to do is to write down these inspirations before he forgets them, will find the idea of canon repugnant. To write a canon a composer needs to plan, and to the inspirationist planning is anathema. He cannot reconcile planning and inspiration so he dismisses canon as mere intellectual trickery without genuine musical worth.

This narrow point of view is really false, but it is astonishing how many people accept it. If one thinks about the matter dispassionately it seems obvious that if composers are to be more than mere musical stenographers, then the making of a piece of music, any piece of music, requires planning. This does not mean that a composer operates on the intellectual-rational level merely; he composes as a whole person whether he is writing a canon or a song. But among other things he thinks! There is no one "natural" way to write music, but if any way of composing could be called "unnatural," it would probably be the weird fantasy that a composer ought to compose *without* using all the intellect he has.

Canons sometimes take time and effort, and "inspired" pieces are supposed to be written in a flash, but it is simply not true that a composition written quickly is, for that reason, more "inspired" than one written slowly. Beethoven took ten years to compose the Ninth Symphony, Mozart wrote his last three symphonies in a summer. A composer might write a canon easily or it might prove a difficult task requiring a great deal of time and thought. Aesthetically, it makes no difference to us how hard the composer had to tussle in order to make the piece; all that matters is the final product. If the music sounds bad, if the song or canon or symphony is botched and poorly made, then it is bad whether it was written in a minute or a lifetime.

VIRTUOSITY, CRAFT AND PLAY

There is another aspect to the epithet, "artificial." Even though some canons are utterly simple to compose, and some are exceedingly difficult, the non-professional may view the whole procedure of canon with suspicion on the grounds that the composer appears to seek out the technically abstruse in order to demonstrate his virtuosity. Canons appear to be harder to make than other musical products and the lay listener is likely to think, "When a thing is so difficult to do as that, maybe the composer is merely showing off, like a juggler who can spin hoops, stand on his head, roll a medicine ball with his feet and play pingpong with the paddle held between his teeth. It's difficult but it's athletics, not music."

This is a natural enough feeling and sometimes it is perfectly justified. It is certainly true that many composers, including Bach, Mozart, Beethoven, Brahms, and Schoenberg, among others, have written canons which are technical rather than essentially musical feats. During the eighteenth century, and well into the nineteenth, it was fashionable to write short canons in letters, autograph books, and the like. These little canons, more like epigrams than anything else, show the composers at play. They delighted in their craft, and these elegant, unpretentious canons gave them pleasure in the same way that a *bon mot* delighted an 18th century literary man.

The four part canon by Bach which we quoted above is an incidental piece of this type. It was probably composed very quickly, for it was written in an autograph book together with the following inscription:

> To contribute this little item at this place to the Honored Owner in the hope of friendly remembrance is the wish of Joh. Sebast. Bach, Court Organist and Chamber Musician to His Saxon Highness.
> Weimar, August 2, 1713.

Bach's little composition is a riddle canon, albeit an extremely easy one to solve. The clue to the solution lies in the four different clefs at the beginning of the canon. Each voice sings the same melody but in a different clef. The points of entry for each of the voices are revealed by the mark, ◊, and the circular nature of the composition is indicated by the signum, 𝒇, which appears at the beginning and end of the melody.

"Canon a 4 Voc: Perpetuus", J. S. Bach

The four different clefs at the beginning are responsible for the four different pitches on which the melody is sung. The treble and bass clefs are well known; the clef sign, ♯, indicates that middle C is on the line enclosed in the clef.

Delight in riddles is a common human trait, and it is not surprising to find that composers have produced riddle canons throughout the centuries and right up to the present day. Indeed, in Medieval times the word canon meant something different from what it means today. The canon (in the literal sense of rule) was the direction for singing the music, and a composer often wrote the rule or canon in an obscure way, challenging the singers to unravel his meaning. The four clefs and the entry signs constitute the canonic inscription for the Bach canon, but sometimes the rule was a sentence or a word. The tenor voice of Dufay's *"Missa L'Homme Armé"* carries the following enigmatic Latin inscription at the beginning of the third Agnus Dei: *"Cancer eat plenus et redeat medius."* (Let the crab proceed full and re-

COUNTERPOINT

turn half.) The singers of the tenor part had to "solve" the sentence to discover that it meant: sing the *cantus firmus* twice, first in full note values then in halved note values but backwards ("return half"); but since the crab's normal motion is backwards, the "proceeding" section must have the melody in reverse, and the "returning" section must sound it in its regular form!

The writing of a single line of music with a rule or direction for making it into a composition of several independent parts was not always a matter of intellectual play or scholastic obscurity. Until the sixteenth century all music had to be copied out laboriously by hand, and even well into the eighteenth century, printed music was less plentiful than we tend to assume. Therefore, any device which permitted a shorthand notation was useful in a practical way. Compare for example, the space needed for the shorthand version of the well-known round, "Row Row Row Your Boat," with the written out version. The singers need only know the melody and when to come in. Voice entries are indicated in the single line version by the sign, ◇, and the written out version is really unnecessary for performance. The single line is thus a condensed version of the music, complete in itself, and with directions for use.

Riddles, delight in craft, virtuosity, technical dis-

Row Row Row Your Boat (Shorthand Version)

play, all appear in abundance in Bach's *Musical Offering*. When the old man went to visit Frederick the Great, the king gave him a theme and asked him to improvise a fugue upon it. This Bach did with great success, and after he had returned to Leipzig he composed another fugue (which, like the first one, he called a ricercar), a trio sonata, and a group of ten canons. He had the whole engraved at his own expense and presented a copy to the king as a musical offering. Every one of the individual compositions uses the royal theme. The work is full of puzzles. Some of the canons are extremely intricate in construction, and appear in the original written in very enigmatic notation. Even the dedication is an acrostic: *Regis Iusso Cantio Et Reliqua Canonica Arte Resoluta* (At the King's Command, the Song and the Remainder Resolved with Canonic Art). The first letter of each of the Latin words spells out "RICERCAR."

The *Musical Offering* demonstrates Bach's virtuosity in a forthright, not to say, blunt manner. He was proud of his craftsmanship (even though he used to say that anyone could do what he did if he would work as hard) and not in the least bashful about demonstrating it. Like a magician's silk hat, the *Musical Offering* is full of curious and beautiful things; and the old prestidigitator draws from it marvel after marvel: the canonic fugue, the four part canon, the canons woven around the theme itself, the sonata to crown all trio sonatas. And when we know the hat must surely be empty, he conjures up the wonder of wonders, the final six part ricercar, a composition for which there are no words at all.

But they are musical, not merely technical marvels. We admire the music, not Bach's sleight-of-hand. The canons speak to us no less than the fugues and trio sonatas, capture us and wind us into their sound worlds, something no technical exercise can do. Playfulness, technical mastery of course, but transformed. The absolute canonic rigor is only the outward sign of the profound inner unity and purity of the music. Technique has been left far behind. We are conscious only of the beauty and splendor of the thing materialized. Truly there is something about canon which, at least in the hands of such a master, is more than epigram, play, puzzle, or technique.

THE MUSICAL EFFECTS OF CANON

The deeper meaning of canon and its validity as a procedure is involved with the whole matter of unity and variety in music. Every melody in a canon is absolutely identical. Unless the canon is accompanied by free voices, the musical fabric is woven entirely from exactly the same kind of threads—to be more accurate, the same thread. All linear events in the music are reducible finally to a single melody, which maintains its abolute integrity in every part. The woven whole has the same sort of repetition-sequence unity which comes about through the use of free imitation, but, in addition, it has this unique unity of melody. There are no loose notes; no melodic tone is sacrificed to the requirements of the vertical organization. Yet everything fits; tones, chords, phrases, all belong together. The formal perfection and the elegance of this type of musical structure is deeply satisfying. In making, and in listening to canons, our desire for aesthetic economy is satisfied. Much comes from little; the variety spreads and blooms from a single melody.

When the follower, or followers, imitate the leader exactly, there is a unity of identity between the voices; but in many other types of canon this identity is stretched. Then we have effects of variety, very much from very little. Consider the following canon from the *Musical Offering*. Here the follower is not identical to the leader but its exact inversion. Leader and follower are in a complex relationship, hence we are conscious above all of the proliferating variety of the music. The unity of the whole is strained because we do not hear the same melody in the second voice. Something not quite new is proferring itself, thus creating tension between leader and follower. But, by maintaining the inversion rigorously, the composer creates a tense, stretched unity between the two voices. The melody of the follower is entirely different from the leader, yet at the same time it is simply its mirror image.

Canon by Inversion, Musical Offering

The canon is 43 bars long. Notice that the bottom voice is the exact inversion of the top voice; it enters at a different beat in the measure than the leader with a consequent conflict in accents between the two voices.

The relationship between leader and follower is even more tenuous in canons such as the following one from Bach's *Art of Fugue*. The follower imitates by inversion, but, at the same time, it moves twice as slowly as the leader. Bach called it *Canone per augmentationem in motu contrario* (canon by augmentation in contrary [inverted] motion). A canon like this has little in common with one in which follower duplicates leader. The whole emphasis of the music is upon variety, to such an extent that it seems to contradict any underlying unity between the two voices. There is even tension between tempos: the first voice moves in a different time world from the second. Yet the two melodies coexist, complement and reinforce each other and make a unity. And ultimately, far below the immediately perceptible level, they are identical.

The bottom voice imitates the leader, only inverted and twice as slowly. Half way through, the slow voice moves to the top and the top voice to the bottom—the music being written in such a way that either voice can serve as a bass to the other. The canon is extremely intricate from the point of view of accent and rhythm, and is absolutely rigorous even though very long, over one hundred measures.

Perhaps the ultimate stretch between leader and follower is to be found in the crab canon. In a canon such as the one just discussed, the two melodies move in different time worlds—one lives twice as fast as the other—but in a crab canon the leader moves forward and the follower imitates the melody but backwards! The two melodies sound as different as possible, having no immediately perceptible relation of identity to each other.

There is an excellent short crab canon in the *Musical Offering*. Considering the top voice as the leader—either voice could be the leader since they begin together—the follower "begins" its imitation at the very end of the composition. The top voice has the melody moving forward and the bottom voice has the same melody, only turned end to end.

Canon by Retrogression (Crab Canon) Musical Offering, J. S. Bach

Dead Center

Such time-defying canons are relatively rare, but some contemporary composers, Hindemith, Schoenberg, and Webern, among others, have shown a new interest in them. Hindemith extends the crab idea even further in his *Ludos Tonalis*. There the whole final Postludium, an extended movement, is identical to the Praeludium, only backwards and upside down. Here are a few measures from the beginning of the Praeludium and their counterpart from the end of the Postludium.

Praeludium, Ludos Tonalis, Paul Hindemith

Postludium, Ludos Tonalis, Paul Hindemith

No contemporary music shows such a preoccupation with canonic devices as that of Anton Webern. His later music proclaims the aesthetic idea of much from little, usually intensified to very much from very little, in its every aspect—melody, harmony, counterpoint, orchestration. It is rigorous motivically, as we showed in the chapter on melodic expansion, and in his later works, harmonically as well. Even the orchestration, the distribution of the instruments, contrasts of tone colors, etc., serves a structural rather than a decorative purpose.

One can find every variety of canon in his music, and often whole movements are canonically constructed. As one might expect, Webern is especially fond of the canonic types in which leader and follower are in a stretched relationship to each other, and crab canon, often combined with inversion, is an excellent procedure for him to realize his rigorous musical ideal. Here follower is completely different from leader, the new is absolutely new, yet at the same time the follower and the leader are in a certain sense identical.

The first variation from the second movement of his Symphony Opus 21 which follows below is typical of Webern's canonic style. The melodies are quite independent, they are consistently dissonant to each other and rhythmically differentiated. Yet they con-

Variation I, Symphony Op. 21, Anton Webern

the structure of music

tinually cross and overlap each other, twining together to form a transparent, elastic texture.

The two middle voices carry out a canon by inversion, while the top and bottom voices have simultaneously another canon by inversion. The whole variation (and of course all the voices) is constructed so that it flows forward to the middle point, then pivots and flows backward to its beginning. Therefore there are symmetries in every direction, a forward and backward mirroring, and an up and down (inversion of the melody) mirroring.

Thus Webern attains the quality of tense, poised balance so characteristic of his later music: it has the wildest, freest imaginable variety, which, paradoxically, is but the sensible manifestation of a calm, transparent, almost absolute and immovable unity.

INTERCHANGEABLE COUNTERPOINT

From time to time in the last chapters I mentioned that certain melodies were written in such a way that either could be the bass for the other; or to put it in another way, the two melodies could be interchanged and the result would be pleasing no matter which voice was on top. When two melodies are written so that this is possible, the result is called double counterpoint. The whole procedure of interchange of melodic lines has been called traditionally, invertible counterpoint; but the word inversion, used in this sense is quite misleading, and the word interchange is less ambiguous and more descriptive.

By means of interchange a new surface of melody may be exposed without disturbing the unity of the music. The following passages from the Duet #4 of Bach's Four Duets are identical except that, in the second, the bottom line is on top and the top line is on the bottom.

Duet #4, Four Duets, J. S. Bach

From: J. S. Bach, 4 Duets (Urtext), Peters Edition No. 4465. With permission of the publishers C. F. Peters Corporation, N. Y.

The second version is certainly different from the first. All of the vertical intervals have changed and some of these changes cause important differences in harmonic meaning, but the essential difference is that of surface. We always hear top voices more easily and our attention is focused on them; thus the melody, which has been there all the time, only down below, suddenly sounds new and fresh when it is brought to the surface.

Interchangeable melodies are a useful means for musical expansion and extension, and composers write them for very practical reasons—indeed for much the same reason that we would buy a reversible topcoat-raincoat. We are able to use the coat in rainy or fair weather, and have in effect two coats in one. The composer's passage of double counterpoint is useful in a similar way—he gets twice as much from the music because he can turn it inside out like the coat.

So for practical reasons, fugue subjects are generally written in double counterpoint with their countersubjects because the composer knows in advance that subject and countersubject will have to appear above and below each other before the fugue is over. Double counterpoint is not limited to fugue; it is useful in almost any contrapuntal texture, and may be found in sonata, dance, and song forms as well.

Quite often the composer will put two of the voices in double counterpoint and include other "free" voices which do not take part in the formal interchange. That is the situation in the excerpt from Beethoven's "Grand Fugue for String Quartet" which follows.

Grand Fugue for String Quartet, Opus 133, Beethoven

Notice that each of the melodies, marked A and B, appears four times, twice on top and twice on the bottom. At measure 273 the slow melody is below, the faster melody above. At measure 280 both melodies are moved a fifth higher (viola and first violin) without being interchanged, while the second violin continues freely. The interchange begins at measure 289 when the slow melody is placed on top (second violin) and the fast melody in the bottom voice (cello). The viola's part, beginning at measure 289, is a free continuation. Finally, at measure 296, the two melodies are transposed up a fifth again, while second violin and cello continue freely.

The passage of double counterpoint is eight measures long. It is repeated on a different pitch level (measure 289), then interchanged and later repeated on a new pitch level again (measure 296). A few small alterations are made when the melodies are moved about, in order to fulfill vertical requirements, but the writing is on the whole quite rigorous. Thus, by means of interchange and transpositions of the melodies, Beethoven was able to expand eight measures of double counterpoint to four times its original length.

TRIPLE COUNTERPOINT

Triple counterpoint works exactly like double counterpoint except that there are many more combinations possible because three voices are involved. In any passage of triple counterpoint, there are theoretically six possible combinations of three melodic lines.

Possible Combinations of Three Melodies (Triple Counterpoint)

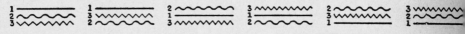

All of the six combinations are seldom used in any single composition, but in a well written triple counterpoint they all could be used, if needed. The composer is always careful to write the passage in such a way that any one of the three voices could serve

as the bottom or the top voice. He knows that if the
melody will work in either of these two exposed positions, it will probably make a satisfactory middle
voice.

Combinations of Triple Counterpoint, Contrapunctus VIII, Art of Fugue, J. S. Bach

In his great triple fugue, Contrapunctus VIII from *The Art of Fugue,* Bach uses the three themes in four of the possible arrangements, repeating the first combination at the very end of the fugue. Except for a few very short episodes the themes themselves are the substance of the final third of the composition. The five combinations from the fugure are given below.

```
1   3   2   3   1
2   1   3   2   2
3   2   1   1   3
```

Diagram of combinations from Contrapunctus VIII, *The Art of Fugue.*

INTERCHANGE AND HARMONY

Melodies can be written in such a way that they may interchange at any interval the composer desires, but the intervals commonly used are those of the octave, tenth, twelfth, and fifteenth. (Tenth equals an octave plus a third, twelfth equals an octave plus a fifth, and fifteenth equals two octaves.) When the counterpoint is in the octave or the fifteenth, the intervallic relations between the two lines are least disturbed; in counterpoint at the tenth or twelfth the changes in harmony are more striking.

The harmonic context, and the whole matter of "right and wrong" harmonic intervals in interchangeable counterpoint, depends upon the particular idiom in which the music is written. The so-called "rules" refer either to the harmonic idiom of Bach, or in the case of some manuals, to an even more restricted ideal corresponding to the practice of no composer who ever lived. Contemporary composers use interchangeable counterpoint in a much more dissonant idiom than either Bach or Beethoven, and their harmonic treatment is naturally quite different.

Walter Piston, in his book, *Counterpoint,* has intimated that a dissonant style makes contrapuntal writing somehow easier. He says in his concluding chapter, "Modern composers have used the contrapuntal devices of canon, inversion and mirror writing. Their effectiveness depends upon the harmonic style adopted for the particular work. If it is a style in which all notes are regarded as consonant together, it is obvious that the contrapuntal combinations pose no problem of technique for the composer."

But no contemporary style in which "all notes are regarded as consonant together" exists. A dissonant style does not necessarily mean that "all notes are regarded as consonant together." Nor does a prevailingly dissonant style make contrapuntal combination easier (or more difficult either) than a prevailingly consonant style. The composer today needs to treat his dissonances with as much care, perhaps more, than the composer of classical times. His problems are different, but he cannot (and to my knowledge no serious contemporary composer does) dispense with the harmonic aspect of the music.

MULTIPLE AND TOTALLY INVERTIBLE COUNTERPOINT

Quadruple, quintuple, and sextuple counterpoint are quite rare species. Double counterpoint is to be found in abundance in the works of most contrapuntal composers, and triple counterpoint is fairly common. But the coda of the finale of Mozart's *Jupiter Symphony* is quite exceptional from the point of view of interchangeable counterpoint, for here Mozart combined all the thematic elements of the movement in a long passage of quintuple counterpoint! An excerpt, with the "filler" instruments left out, is below.

In this amazing display, with themes now bubbling up to the surface, now sinking into inner parts, the principle of interchangeable counterpoint is strikingly illustrated. Everything combines with everything else; any voice can function as a top or bottom or middle voice. The five fragments form and reform into new patterns, constantly expanding in a kaleidoscopic interplay of elements.

Interchange of parts may be combined with other contrapuntal procedures too. Bach's experiments in

The thematic fragments are numbered from one to five. Naturally not all the possible combinations are utilized. The original quintuple counterpoint is only four measures long; illustrated above are four and one half repetitions of it, each time with the melodies in a different position in relation to each other. The effect here is quite like imitation because the fragments are so short and because the interchanges follow each other immediately.

The Art of Fugue and the *Musical Offering,* where he interchanged voices and inverted them as well, remain fairly isolated from ordinary contrapuntal practice. The totally invertible fugues from *The Art of Fugue,* though hardly typical of any general musical practice, are masterpieces of interchangeable counterpoint.

Bach wrote two sets of them. Each is constructed in

Contrapunctus XVIIIa and Contrapunctus XVIIIb, Art of Fugue

© E. F. Kalmus, Inc.

Here is the ending of Contrapunctus XVIIIa with its mirror companion, Contrapunctus XVIIIb.

such a way that the whole fugue can be turned upside down: the soprano line becomes bass; alto becomes tenor; tenor becomes alto; bass becomes soprano. Not only that, but each of the lines, when it
is interchanged, is inverted. The result is a completely new composition which is brought into existence by flipping over the entire piece. One fugue is
the exact mirror image of the other.

Not the least astonishing aspect of this *tour de
force* is the fact that when the fugues are inverted
they remain in the key of D minor, the tonal home
base for the whole *Art of Fugue*. There is not the
slightest sense of strain about the compositions either.
All four are easy, good humored, and imbued with
that ordered calm to be found in all of Bach's late
works. Indeed he himself must have been quite delighted with them, because he made a two-keyboard
version of Contrapunctus XVI, weaving a free fourth
voice into the texture of the original three voice fugue,
demonstrating in a most practical way that this was
"ear-music," not "eye-music."

So much of the contrapuntal music we hear has a woven, imitative texture, free or strict, that we may easily assume that imitation is *the* contrapuntal procedure. Such a view would not only be incomplete, but might give a false impression about the nature of counterpoint itself. A large portion of the music written before the sixteenth century and during the twentieth century is rooted in other principles, and imitative procedures alone while they have dominated the scene at certain moments of history, have never been the *only* contrapuntal means available to composers.

Cantus firmus writing, already touched upon somewhat in the chapter on melody, was the dominant procedure from the very beginnings of Western polyphony until about the middle of the fifteenth century; and the principle involved, the writing of new melodies around the framework of a given fixed melody, has never been lost, appearing in one form or another in such diverse musical types and forms as motet and mass, divisions on a ground, chaconne, passacaglia, chorale prelude and chorale variations. Even today's jazz improvisations on a popular tune make use of the principle.

Cantus firmus writing is the oldest of all contrapuntal procedures. To the first composers of polyphony the idea of superimposing a new melody on an old familiar one must have seemed quite natural. The new ornamental line, superimposed upon the *cantus firmus,* enhanced the given melody, presenting it without changing it fundamentally.

The notion of superposition is a thoroughly linear conception. Indeed the ancients had no other conception of a musical organism. The idea of a chord, in our sense, did not exist in the eleventh, twelfth and thirteenth centuries; the only way they could conceive of a two or three voice composition was as a group of superimposed melodies.

In many ways the early compositions, especially in the decorative and ornamental character of the freshly composed lines, and their dependence upon a rigid *cantus firmus,* reflect some of the literary practices of medieval times; and it is well to remember that almost all of the written music was liturgical, and grew out of the word-orientated chant of the church. The literary practice of commentary upon a given text was popular, and very often the commentary and the given text appear together in contemporary manuscripts. Sometimes the commentary is in the margin and sometimes it appears interlined with the original text. Moreover, there are quite a few literary manuscripts which include the original text, its commentary, and a commentary upon the commentary.

More influential on the art of music was the medieval literary practice of troping. Sometime during the eighth century it became popular to insert words, phrases, and in some instances whole poems between the words of the authorized texts. For example, the authorized text for the *Kyrie* of the mass was expanded from *Kyrie eleison* to *Kyrie fons bonitatis eleison.* An even longer interpolation: *Kyrie fons pietatis, a quo bona cuncta procedunt eleison.* The interpolations were explanations of, or commentary upon the fixed official texts, and were fitted to monodic (single line, unaccompanied) chants.

In modern times the practice of troping has been revived by James Joyce, especially in his *Finnegans Wake,* where borrowed materials, familiar songs, poems and sayings are expanded, commented upon and often distorted by interpolated material. Frequently Joyce's interpolations are in a different language from the borrowed text, a device which helps to keep the borrowed and the new separate from each other and more or less decipherable. Bilingual tropes were fairly common in medieval times, too. The quotations above are in Greek and Latin, in this case almost by accident, as these are the only Greek words in the canon of the mass, but liturgical texts were troped in French-over-Latin and German-over-Latin as well.

Many medieval musical compositions can be readily understood as musical tropes. If one singer sang the original text and music and at the same time another singer sang a new melody with a new text explaining or commenting upon the *cantus firmus,* the result would be a vertical trope. Instead of being interpolated the troped words (and a melody to go with them) were superimposed to make text and commentary available simultaneously. Some of the finest medieval compositions are tropes of this type.

Below is the beginning of a two voice trope on the words and melody, *Benedicamus Domino.*

The principle involved in the vertical trope below, extended and adapted in various ways, was the chief contrapuntal procedure for several hundred years. Composing consisted chiefly of inventing new melodies to go with pre-existing ones, and the whole was built up by a process of accretion, layer by layer. It is difficult for us to imagine a composer writing one voice of the music at a time, but that was their method. Over a given melody they composed a new one, and even if the composition were to have three or four voices they still composed them successively.

As long as the one-after-another method of composition was in use a *cantus firmus* was almost indispensable—one had to begin with something! But during the fifteenth century new ideas, especially imitative procedures, came into fashion, and the whole three- or four-hundred-year-old tradition of *cantus firmus* writing was gradually abandoned. Okeghem lived at a time when new procedures were rapidly becoming popular; indeed his contemporary, Obrecht, is one of the first masters of imitative style. Okeghem knew about imitative writing, and in his song settings he used the procedure fluently, but in his masses he held closer to conservative traditions. The following excerpt from his *L'Homme Armé* mass is interesting because it shows medieval *cantus firmus* writing at its ripest. Josquin, and later Palestrina, wrote *cantus firmus* masses too, but in their treatments the *cantus firmus* is no longer in any sense a fundamental re-

Stirps Je - se flo - ri - ge - ram germi - na - vit vir - gu - lam, et in flo - re spi - ri - tus

Be— — — — — — — — — — — — — — —

qui - e - scit pa - ra - cli - - - tus fru - ctum pro - fert vir - -

- — — — ne — — — — — — — — — — — —

gu - la per quem vi - vunt sae - cu - la,

- - di - - - - ca - - mus

stir - pis ex Da - vi - ti - cae, vir - ga di - cta my - sti - ce *etc.*

— Do - - - - - - - (mino)

The rhythm is unmeasured and therefore very free. Because of the exuberant welling up of melody in the troping upper voice the speed of the *cantus firmus* is relatively very slow, and each long note becomes something like a drone. Notice that changes of pitch in the *cantus firmus* often occur at or near cadence points.

quirement of the music. They are "late" composers bowing gracefully toward a long musical tradition.

It is almost certain that Okeghem no longer composed in the medieval fashion of successive layers. There are many long passages where the *cantus firmus* rests, and although he was certainly not the first composer to swing free of the *cantus firmus*, it is obvious in the music below that he is no longer dependent upon it in the way that the eleventh and twelfth century composers were. What he did—and this is generally true of all his *cantus firmus* masses, was to absorb the *cantus firmus* into the musical web by having all of the voices move in roughly similar time values. The *cantus firmus* is one voice among many, and the web of sound has a relatively homogeneous quality in sharp contrast to the stratified sound of earlier compositions.

Of course the other voices are not troping the *cantus firmus* in the medieval sense at all; as a matter of fact, the *cantus firmus* is really a popular tune of the day, and any liturgical significance between *cantus firmus* and the other voices has vanished completely. The *cantus firmus* functions as an abstract, structural unifier. It appears in every movement of the Ordinary of the mass: once in the *Kyrie*, twice in the *Gloria*, three times in the *Credo* (once incomplete), once in the *Sanctus* and once in the *Agnus Dei*. It is hardly the "theme" of the mass, but in an entirely abstract way serves as the foundation upon which the superstructure of voices is erected. In the absence of imitative texture, strongly profiled motives, short, clearly defined phrases, the *cantus firmus* is the only "binder" element in the freely expanding organism. Its presence allows the other lines to unfold freely and independently in the old medieval manner of which Okeghem was perhaps the last great exponent.

Credo from Missa l'Homme Armé, Okeghem

The *cantus firmus* appears in the bottom voice and is underlined with a heavy line. Note how the segments of the *cantus firmus* are separated by long rests, and how its note values correspond closely to those of the other voices. The *L'Homme Armé* tune is quite a long one; represented here is the first phrase, and at the very end of the excerpt, the beginning of the second phrase.

175   COUNTERPOINT

The seventeenth and eighteenth century Protestant chorale prelude was a new form adapted to the liturgy of the Protestant church, but its roots went far back into the middle ages. The liturgical purpose of the chorale prelude was to familiarize the congregation with the hymn of the day, and the organist usually presented the hymn tune surrounded by an imaginative web of polyphony. The *cantus firmus* type of chorale prelude, in which the hymn tune is presented in long note values, was quite popular, and many of Bach's chorale preludes are of that type.

In a certain sense Bach, in his chorale preludes, revived the medieval practice of vertical troping; that is, he so constructed the melodies surrounding the *cantus firmus* that they illuminated the meaning of the words of the chorale. Attempts have been made, notably by Schweitzer and Pirro, to read very specific meanings into the melodic figures and the rhythms, skips, steps, etc., comprising them. It is all too easy to read into music what one wants to hear, and Schweitzer and Pirro probably went too far in their interpretations, but there is no doubt that the melodic web accompanying the *cantus firmus* illuminates the mood of the words of the chorale in a general way. Thus in the chorale prelude, *"Durch Adam's Fall ist ganz verderbt"* (Through Adam's Fall Mankind Fell Too), the chromatic character of the melodies in the upper voices and the chromatic skips in the bass line create an atmosphere of tension, even though one might not want to accept the specific interpretation of the downward skips in the bass line as literal illustrations of "falling."

Chorale Prleude, Durch Adam's Fall ist ganz verderbt, J. S. Bach

From: J. S. Bach, Complete Organ Works, Vol. V, Peters Ed. No. 244 with permission of the publishers, C. F. Peters Corp., N. Y.

The chorale tune appears in the top voice as a *cantus firmus*. Each of the other voices has its own typical rhythmic figures, but all three accompanying voices are quite chromatic. The downward bass skips not only cover a wide range, most of them are chromatic skips.

Bach's *cantus firmus* treatment was quite different from that of Okeghem or the eleventh and twelfth century composers. He usually surrounded the *cantus firmus* with an imitative web. In the excerpt quoted above each line is motivically fairly independent of the others—each has its own typical motives and rhythms—but in the passage from *"Erscheinen ist der herrliche Tag"* (The Glorious Day Has Dawned) which follows, the structure depends more heavily upon imitative procedures.

The use of one or more contrapuntal procedures in a composition does not necessitate the exclusion of others. Bach was perfectly capable of writing a complete fugue over a *cantus firmus*, and the canonic treatment of the *cantus firmus*, which he carried to

Chorale Prelude, Erscheinen ist der herrliche Tag, J. S. Bach

From J. S. Bach, Complete Organ Works, Vol. V, Peters Ed. No. 244 with permission of the publishers, C. F. Peters Corp., N. Y.

The two inner voices have the same motivic material and are treated in free imitation at phrase beginnings. The *cantus firmus,* which appears in the top and bottom voices, is in canon with itself throughout.

Variation I, Canonic Variations over Vom Himmel Hoch, J. S. Bach

From: J. S. Bach, Complete Organ Works, Vol V, Peters Ed. No. 244 with permission of the publishers, C. F. Peters Corp., N. Y.

such heights, was nothing new at his time. The composers of the fifteenth century had put the *cantus firmus* through every conceivable contrapuntal treatment long before him.

The combining of canon with *cantus firmus* treatment is pushed to its outer limits in Bach's *Canonic Variations on the Christmas chorale, Vom Himmel hoch da komm' ich her* (From Heaven Above to Earth I come). This is a series of five elaborations, each a different type of canon, and each having for its *cantus firmus* the chorale tune. The chorale is treated in the first three variations as: canon at the octave over the chorale; canon at the fifth over the chorale; canon at the seventh over the chorale. The fourth variation has a canon by augmentation over the chorale tune, too. The fifth and final variation treats the chorale tune differently. The phrases of the tune are broken up and the chorale fragments themselves are placed in canon: at the sixth, at the second, at the third, by inversion and in diminution. On the facing page is the opening of the first variation, one of the warmest, gayest pieces Bach ever wrote.

By the late eighteenth century the chorale prelude was a thing of the past, so far as its vitality as a form is concerned. Mozart, who put it to a theatrical use in his opera, *The Magic Flute*, where the two men in armor sing to the old chorale, "*Ach Gott vom Himmel sieh darein*," probably knew some of Bach's chorale preludes; and Beethoven, in the slow movement of his A Minor string quartet, certainly had in mind the typical *cantus firmus* treatment of the chorale prelude. Brahms revived interest in the form and wrote some excellent ones, modeling them after the Bach tradition.

One of the most interesting of contemporary *cantus*

firmus compositions is Ernst Krenek's *Five Prayers, For Women's Chorus.* It has some characteristics similar to medieval compositions and others, especially the personal expressiveness, more reminiscent of Bach's approach. Like the composers of medieval times Krenek uses two texts and so adjusts them that one tropes the other vertically. His *cantus firmus* carries the words of the *Pater Noster* in Latin. After

Through Thy Submitting All, Five Prayers, Ernst Krenek

© American Inst. of Musicology in Rome.

the structure of music

the *cantus firmus* has been sung monodically the composer breaks it into five separate segments, one for each of the five prayers, the texts for which are from poems by the Elizabethan poet, John Donne.

Donne's poems have been so arranged by the composer that they trope the *Pater Noster;* moreover, by his control over the placement of the two texts, and by his musical treatment of them, Krenek is able to interpret both texts, and to infuse the music with a distinctly personal expression which has much in common with Bach's intensely personal interpretations of chorale tunes.

The treatment of the *cantus firmus* in the above excerpt as well as throughout the composition, is more in the manner of the fifteenth century than Bach. Rhythm and accent are quite free and irregular, as in Okeghem and Dufay, and like the *L'Homme Armé* mass the *cantus firmus* acts as a binder to unify the whole. However, the supporting melodies do not have the individual freedom of Okeghem's. Most generally these three melodic lines are put in opposition to the *cantus firmus*. The *cantus firmus* itself is set in longer note values to isolate it effectively, and although there are imitative entries here and there, the other voices are most often treated more like a single homogeneous entity.

Of all constructive principles in music none seems quite so rigid as isorhythm, a procedure common in the thirteenth and fourteenth century motets and polyphonic song settings. "Iso" is the Greek root meaning "one," and an isorhythmic composition has one or more voices which adhere rigidly to a single rhythm pattern. Typically the rhythmic pattern is long and quite complex.

In the isorhythmic compositions of the thirteenth and fourteenth centuries the *cantus firmus* voice, usually the tenor, was always isorhythmic. The long rhythm pattern was repeated at least once, often several times. The other voices were composed, one after another, around the isorhythmic *cantus firmus*. Here is a simple isorhythmic melodic line, the tenor voice of the *Kyrie I* from the mass by Guillaume Machaut, who was the most famous musician-poet of fourteenth century France.

Tenor voice of first Kyrie from Mass in Four Voices, Guillaume Machaut

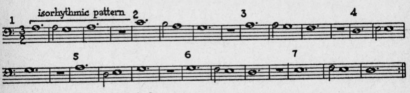

© American Inst. of Musicology in Rome.

The rhythm pattern occurs seven times, each time with a different pitch contour. The rhythm alone, not the melody as a melodic-rhythmic whole, is the organizing force. This isorhythmic tenor has a relatively simple pattern (talea); usually the pattern is much more extended.

The fact that a *cantus firmus* is isorhythmic is not so striking, especially when compared with the *cantus firmus* treatment of Okeghem and Dufay, but when all the voices in a composition are isorhythmic, as in the following *Ite Missa Est* section from the same mass, the peculiar organizing power of iso-

Ite Missa Est, from Mass in Four Voices, Machaut

The rhythms of the bottom voices of A and A' are identical. This is true also of the tenor voice in A and A'. The top two voices are freely iso-rhythmic—that is with slight variations.

rhythm is revealed dramatically. The music has been copied in such a way that the rhythmic relationships are easy to see. The rhythm pattern is eight measures long and there is one repeat. The repeat is labeled A'. The rhythm patterns of each of the voices are identical in A and A'. The bottom voice of the A section has the same rhythm as the bottom voice of A'. The two tenor voices are identical rhythmically, too. Some liberties are taken in the upper voices, but they are clearly isorhythmic in construction.

The melodic contour for each voice is different in A and A'; in fact one can hardly perceive the likenesses between A and A' because of these melodic differences. Rhythmically the music is extremely rigid in construction, yet so far as the pitch contour of the melodies is concerned it is very free. To the ear there is no rigidity at all, there is only the feeling of an exuberant, thick growth of melody, mysteriously organized, and "rational" on some level below immediate perception.

Parallel to the idea of isorhythmic construction is the conception of an isomelic organization, that is, construction with a "single melody." When the isomelic and isorhythmic principles are brought together some astounding musical results ensue.

To explain the procedure simply, let us manufacture a very short rhythmic pattern: ♩ ♪♪ ♪. Now if we superimpose this five note rhythmic pattern upon a longer pitch pattern, such as this one containing six tones, , the result will be a continuously varied melodic line, absolutely rigid in both melody and rhythm, isomelic and isorhythmic. If pitch pattern and rhythm pattern are so arranged that they begin together, the repetition of the rhythm will begin before the pitch pattern is complete, and the patterns will overlap until the rhythm pattern has been repeated six times and the pitch pattern five.

In practice the isorhythmic and isomelic patterns are longer than this. The tenor voice from the following anonymous fourteenth century motet is a good example of how the two procedures were used to-

Tenor of Anonymous 14th C. Motet (After Bessler & Reese) Alma Redemptoris Mater

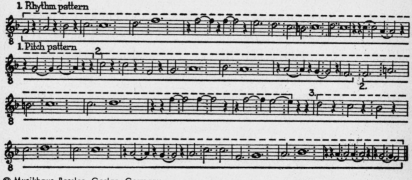

gether. There are three repetitions of the rhythm pattern and two of the pitch pattern. The pitch pattern is taken from the well known Gregorian chant, *"Alma Redemptoris Mater."*

Apparently the composer felt that the "authority" of the tune was preserved even when he clothed it in a different rhythmic garb at its second appearance. In the manipulating and adapting of the given material the treatment is not unlike the way Bach made his chorale tunes into canons, fugue subjects, etc., and used them in diminution, augmentation and inversion.

The *"Alma Redemptoris"* melody is not easy to detect when it is repeated, but it is not completely distorted rhythmically. However it does not need to be heard as a primary melody in the music. Its function

Cantata #11, Final Movement, Webern

Notice that the accent patterns of the various voices are in continual conflict with each other. Word accents as well as purely musical accents help to keep these conflicts sensible, but each voice is a law unto itself so far as placing of the accent is concerned.

is abstract and structural; it is the rocklike foundation upon which the other voices are erected one after the other.

Such "unhearable" methods of organization, though perfectly acceptable musically and aesthetically, have been out of fashion for a long time, and the whole matter might have only a curiosity value except for the fact that some contemporary composers have written music along similar lines.

The final movement from Anton Webern's Second Cantata has an organization remarkably like the isorhythmic and isomelic motets and mass movements of the fourteenth century. At first glance it appears to be a four voice canon, but the melodies do not duplicate each other exactly, the effect is more like that of free imitation. There is no imitation in the ordinary sense, yet the whole composition has such a remarkable consistency that it invites close analysis.

Complete Soprano Line, Cantata #11, Final Movement, Anton Webern

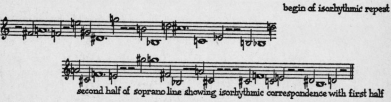

begin of isorhythmic repeat

second half of soprano line showing isorhythmic correspondence with first half

Rhythmically, all of the voices are identical. The entrances are staggered in such a way that the effect is of a rhythmic canon in four voices.

Rhythmic canons are nothing new, but this movement is more than a rhythmic canon, each single voice is isorhythmic too. There is one repetition of the pattern, as in the *"Ite Missa Est"* from the Machaut mass. The complete soprano line, with the isorhythmic repeat shown below it, is on page 187.

The repetition of the pattern is not absolutely exact, but it is too close to be a mere coincidence. Webern places the repetition in such a way that the effect is of variation, the new unfolding out of the old, rather than static identical repetition. Like the older isorhythmic composers, he too cuts the melody into short segments, separated from each other by rests.

Within the line there are certain rhythmic symmetries, brought about by the recurrence of the figures, ♩ ♩· ♩, and ♩ ♩ ♩ ♩. They are not systematic but they tend to give unity to the rhythmic structure.

The composition is isomelic, but in a very curious

Comparison of Soprano and Bass, Cantata #11, Final Movement, Anton Webern

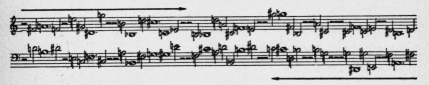

way. The pitch sequence, but not the melodic contour, of the bass line is identical to that of the soprano, only backwards. The soprano line below begins F♯, A, F, E, G♯, D♯, G, etc. Compare this to the bass line, starting from the end of the line. It too, has the sequence F♯, A, F, E, G♯, D♯, G, etc.

The sequence of pitches is the same but the melodic contour is entirely different in each case because the pitches have been used to create different melodies. For example, in the soprano line, from F♯ we go *up* to A and back down to F; at the corresponding point in the bass line, we go (still reading it backwards) from F♯ *down* to A and back up to F. This happens throughout the two melodies as well as in the other two voices, alto and tenor, which are in the same relation of original pitch sequence and backwards pitch sequence.

This condition of extreme melodic freedom is maintained throughout the whole piece, and is complicated by continuous crossings of the four voices, and the highly irregular distribution of accents. There are no clearly defined melodic motives, although now and again one hears fleeting references, sounding almost accidental, between voices.

Such melodic freedom might seem to be mere chaos, and it would be except for the fact that the whole composition is isomelic on another level, too: each melody line is not only related to another by this retrograde pitch sequence idea, but is itself governed by a never-changing pitch sequence of twelve

different tones. This isomelic pitch sequence appears in its inverted and retrograde forms, and transposed

to various pitch levels. The soprano line, for example, is made up of the three statements of the pitch sequence, first in its original form, then transposed a diminished fifth higher, then backwards and inverted.

The isorhythmic and isomelic construction, absolutely rigid in every voice, mirrors the frame of mind and outlook of the composers of the thirteenth and fourteenth centuries. In their music, and in Webern's, the elements of freedom and rigidity are combined; in both types of music there is a tension between these elements. In both one feels the constructive drive as an expression of the belief that above all else, art is a making.

Less austere in conception, and more familiar to modern audiences is the way in which Alban Berg has adapted isorhythmic construction to a dramatic use in his opera, *Wozzeck*. The third scene of Act III, a tavern episode, is based entirely upon the following rhythm pattern:

This rhythm pattern is always present in one or more of the voices like an *ideé fixe*. Its constant repetition screws up the dramatic tension to an almost unbearable intensity. However, the treatment is so subtle and there is so much rhythmic variation that the listener is seldom immediately aware of the pattern itself. It is present like a sensed danger (and this is exactly why Berg chose the procedure for this scene) "felt" but not consciously identified.

In addition to its original form the pattern appears in time values twice and four times as long (augmented and doubly augmented), and in time values twice as short (diminished). Its position in the meas-

ure is continually shifted, thus giving it a new metrical twist; it is changed by different time signatures; and as the climax of the scene is approached several of the variants of the pattern are superimposed to create a tense and dramatic rhythmic structure. Some

COUNTERPOINT

The rhythm pattern is marked by brackets. Note that the pattern does not always begin on the first note of a measure—it is often displaced and syncopated against itself, and at two points the regular form and its augmentation are superimposed. As in the Machaut mass excerpt only the rhythm pattern remains fixed, the melodies are continually varied.

of the variants appear on page 191 above, and the passage shows how Berg superimposed several variants of the pattern to create a complex but coherent rhythmic-metric design.

OSTINATO

Berg called the scene just quoted an "Invention On a Rhythm." It is exactly that, but at the same time its strict isorhythmic construction recalls the isorhythmic motets and mass movements of the thirteenth and fourteenth centuries.

But Berg was not imitating an old form. The rhythm pattern is not completely imperceptible, and the listener feels it on some level throughout the

Finale (excerpt) String Quartet #5, Bela Bartok

The *ostinato* is held in the bass voice for 31 measures. Then it moves to other voices. The figures in the first violin part do not have enough identity to be considered as *ostinati;* they are heard as simple accompaniment figures.

193   COUNTERPOINT

whole scene. The pattern has the character of an *ostinato*. (An *ostinato* is a short, clearly defined melodic phrase which is repeated persistently. The word *ostinato* has the same root as the English word, obstinate.) The thing which distinguishes an *ostinato* from the kind of rhythmic patterns found in the old isorhythmic motets is its perceptibility. Berg's treatment of his rhythm pattern in this scene (twisting it, diminishing and augmenting it) is reminiscent of isorhythmic procedures but the treatment also has much in common with the *ostinato* basses of the seventeenth and eighteenth centuries, and the *ostinato* writing of such contemporaries as Stravinsky, Bartok and Schoenberg.

The short *ostinato* figure in the cello part of the excerpt from Bartok's Fifth String Quartet is quite characteristic. It is so short and it is repeated so incessantly that it can hardly be missed.

A slightly longer *ostinato* figure underlies the whole

First Movement, String Quartet #3, Arnold Schoenberg

the structure of music

of the first movement of Schoenberg's Third String Quartet. Schoenberg does not hold rigidly to the figure throughout the movement: the *ostinato* appears in various transformations, rhythmic, metric and melodic, but its identity is never lost. The opening measures of the movement are given on page 194.

GROUND BASS

A ground bass is an *ostinato* which appears in the bottom voice, and which is able to serve as the foundation for chord progressions. Ground basses were the most popular form of *ostinati* during the period of tonality (1600-1900), and came into fashion as medieval *cantus firmus* writing disappeared. One of the finest early examples is by Claudio Monteverdi, the first great opera composer, who wrote at the turn of the sixteenth and seventeenth centuries—the duet from his opera, *The Coronation of Poppea,* built on a ground bass only four notes long.

Notice that there are no gaps between the successive repetitions of the ground bass; it is simply repeated over and over while the upper voices weave continuous lines above it. The *basso ostinato* gives structure to the music in two different ways: by its being there, that is, by continuous repetition; and by functioning as a harmonic bass line. The harpsichord player had no written out music for the performance, but improvised his part from the harmonies implied by the bass line, according to the rules of

Duet from The Coronation of Poppea, Claudio Monteverdi (after Schering)

Both harpsichordist and bass violist used the bottom line, the *ostinato*. The harpsichordist improvised chords above the ground bass according to the rules of thorough bass.

thorough-bass. The fact that the bass line could be harmonized in various ways allowed for the requisite variety.

From the conception of a ground bass supporting and sustaining upper voices to the idea of variations on a ground bass is only a short step. The English of the seventeenth century were the great masters of such variations on a ground; and of all the English, Henry Purcell was the greatest composer of variations on a *basso ostinato*. The procedure is to be found everywhere in his works, operas, choruses, keyboard music. He was so fond of it that it is almost a mark of his style.

Two variations from the Chaconne movement of his keyboard Suite in G Minor will serve to show how he worked.

The *basso ostinato* is four measures long, but even within the four measures there are symmetries: the same rhythmic figure,  appears three times, giving the whole an easily perceptible profile. There are seventeen variations on the *basso ostinato*,

Chaconne (excerpt) from Suite in G Minor, Henry Purcell

some of which are double, with the *ostinato* repeated. Notice that the variations are quite continuous. One variation leads directly into another and there are no pauses between variations. Throughout the composition, which is quite long, Purcell holds to the original form of the *ostinato* quite rigidly, but there are a few variants; in one variation he puts it in the top voice, and in another he passes it back and forth between the two voices.

The title of the piece, Chaconne, should be explained. By chaconne, Purcell meant variations on a ground. Passacaglias are often variations on *bassi ostinati*, too, but there exist chaconnes and passacaglias which *are not* variations on ground basses, and this makes for confusion. The confusion arises because there are two related but different types of continuous variation. One type, the one in which we are interested, consists of variations over *a melody which is always or almost always in the bottom voice*. The other type consists of continuous variations over a chord progression. The melody of the bass voice may be different for every variation, because the composition is organized by chord progression, not melodic *basso ostinato*. The chaconne for violin alone, by J. S. Bach is the most famous example of this type. It has been suggested that the term, chaconne, be restricted to continuous variations over a chord progression and that all *basso ostinato* continuous variations be called passacaglias. Unfortunately, Bach, Purcell, and all the rest are dead. They named their pieces and they can hardly change them now to satisfy the classifiers.

Variation IV from Passacaglia in C Minor, J. S. Bach

the structure of music

Bach's Passacaglia in C Minor is much larger in scope than Purcell's Chaconne. The *basso ostinato* is eight measures long and there are twenty continuous variations. To finish off the passacaglia, Bach takes the *basso ostinato* itself as a subject and concludes with a long double fugue.

The *ostinato* is in the bass voice most of the time, but in the eleventh, twelfth and thirteenth variations it appears in the upper voices. The fourteenth and fifteenth variations are made up of toccata-like broken chords, but in the fourteenth at least, the *ostinato* is quite obvious. This group of five variations provides a relief from the constant reiteration of the *ostinato* in the bass voice and acts as a sort of middle section for the passacaglia.

Much freer in treatment is Berg's monumental passacaglia from the first act of *Wozzeck*. Berg has as an *ostinato* a series of twelve different tones:

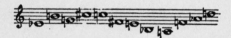

This sequence of pitches is almost always maintained, but in each variation the melodic *ostinato* receives a new rhythmic dress. Since the theme always appears in new rhythms it is much harder to follow than in the passacaglias and chaconnes. But Berg's passacaglia is so long that rhythmic variation is a necessity.

The *ostinato*, although it sometimes appears in the bass voice, is not conceived as a carrier of harmonies.

It is therefore somewhat like a *cantus firmus*—one whose rhythmic character is ever-changing and which is at times heavily ornamented and obscured.

Because of the changes of rhythm some of the variations are short, others quite long. Moreover, some of them are complex and the *ostinato* is quite hidden in the contrapuntal web. The twelfth variation, short and relatively simple, has more in common with the older passacaglias than most of the others, and serves at the same time to illustrate Berg's phenomenal contrapuntal skill.

12th Variation, Passacaglia from Wozzeck, Alban Berg (solo violin and solo cello parts have been omitted)

The musical texture is not so complex as it looks at first glance. Celeste and harp have parts of an accompanying nature, and are so soft that they move into the background. The *ostinato,* played by the trumpet, is clearly audible. Oboe and bassoon imitate its beginning. Wozzeck sings an independent line against it.

The procedures we have discussed are to be found everywhere in music. They are a part of the equipment of every composer. Every performer needs a thorough understanding of them in order to interpret contrapuntal music properly. Listener and amateur may profit from an acquaintance with them. But it is so easy to point them out, to compare them and to relate them to each other, that one can easily mistake them for counterpoint itself.

The procedures are not the music. They are ways of working, and the composer, not the procedure, makes the music. A canon may be perfectly strict and still be worthless. A fugue may be packed with countersubjects, interchangeable counterpoint, cunning strettos and other devices, yet sound dull as dishwater.

Conversely, a composition may use no "standard" procedures at all, nothing we can abstract and attach a label to, yet be truly contrapuntal—because in the balance of the lines, at once independent and dependent, forming a larger whole, yet each contributing its perfect wholeness, is the essence of counterpoint.

Analysis and discussion may help us to understand the procedures, at least in an intellectual way, but to feel *these* relations only the ear is of use.

INDEX